THE
INTRARELIGIOUS
DIALOGUE

R. PANIKKAR

PAULIST PRESS
New York, N.Y./Ramsey, N.J.

Library of Congress
Catalog Card Number: 78-58962

ISBN: 0-8091-0273-0

Published by Paulist Press
Editorial Office: 1865 Broadway, New York, N.Y. 10023
Business Office: 545 Island Road, Ramsey, N.J. 07446

Printed and bound in the
United States of America

ACKNOWLEDGMENTS

Grateful acknowledgment is made to the editors and publishers of the following books and journals for granting permission to use material that appeared in them.

II. 'Fe y creencia. Sobre la experiencia multireligiosa. Un fragmento autobiográfico objetivado'. *Homenaje a Xavier Zubiri* (Madrid: Editorial Moneda y Crédito, 1970, vol. II). A shorter version appeared as: 'A Multireligious Experience. An Objectified Autobiographical Fragment'. *Anglican Theological Review*, vol. LIII, No. 4 (October 1971).

III. 'The Rules of the Game in the Religious Encounter', *The Journal of Religious Studies* (Punjabi University), vol. III, No. 1 (Spring 1971).

IV. 'The Internal Dialogue—The Insufficiency of the So-called Phenomenological "Epoché" in the Religious Encounter', *Religion and Society*, vol. XV, No. 3 (1968).

V. 'The Category of Growth in Comparative Religion: A Critical Self-Examination', *The Harvard Theological Review*, vol. 66, No. 1 (January 1973).

VI. 'Śūnyatā and Plērōma: The Buddhist and Christian Response to the Human Predicament', *Religion and the Humanizing of Man*, edited by J.M. Robinson (Waterloo, Canada: Council on the Study of Religion, 1972).

TABLE OF CONTENTS

v

List of Abbreviations

BU   Brhadarânka Upanisad
BG   Bhagavad Gîtâ
BS   Brahma Sûtra
MB   Mahâbhârata
P.G.   Migne, J.P. Patrologia Cursus Completus. Series Graeca (Paris: Migne, 1857-1866)
P.L.   Migne, J.P. Patrologia Cursus Completus. Series Latina (Paris: Migne, 1844-1855)
RV   Rg Veda
SU   Svetâśvatara Upanisad

For the Bible the usual abbreviations are employed.

PREFACE

There is a long way, painful, but at the same time purifying, that is leading contemporary Christian consciousness from a self-understanding as being a historically privileged people, bearing an exclusive or inclusive message of salvation for the entire world, to an awareness of self-identity that without weakening the strength of a conviction of uniqueness and fidelity to its own calling does make room for different ultimate and salvific human experiences.

For thirty years the author has written extensively on such problems. The present essays are here gathered as stepping stones of that way. They were written in the middle of the internal struggle of the ecclesial self-reflection. They have been detached from another collection of studies, *Myth, Faith and Hermeneutics*, because although they complement the chapters of the other book, their internal unity appears clearer as an independent volume.

R.P.
Santa Barbara, Advent 1977

A Dominique de Ménil

à qui l'expérience multireligieuse
lui a apporté l'approfondissement de son identité,
car la *communio* humaine
est *communicatio in sacris,*

d.d.d.

R.P.

THE INTRARELIGIOUS DIALOGUE

"Accidit ut post dies aliquot, forte ex diuturna continuata meditatione, visio quaedam eidem zeloso manifestaretur, ex qua elicuit quod paucorum sapientium omnium talium diversitatum quae in religionibus per orbem observantur peritia pollentium unam posse facilem quandam concordantiam reperiri, ac per eam in religione perpetuam pacem convenienti ac veraci medio constitui."

Nicolai de Cusa
De Pace seu Concordantia Fidei, I, 1 +

"It happened after some days, perhaps as the fruit of an intense and sustained meditation, that a vision appeared to this ardently devoted Man. In this vision it was manifested that by means of a few sages versed in the variety of religions that exist throughout the world it could be possible to reach a certain peaceful concord. And it is through this concord that a lasting peace in religion may be attained and established by convenient and truthful means."

+Cf. R. Llull, *Liber de quinque sapientibus* expressing the same idea almost two centuries before (apud N. de Cusa, *Opera omnia,,* vol VII *De pace fidei,* ed. R. Klibansky and H. Bascour (Hamburg, Meiner), 1970, pp. 3-4.

"... e aquí preseren comiat los tres savis la un de l'altre molt amablement e molt agradable; e cascú qués perdó a l'altre si havia dita contra sa lig nulla vilana paraula; e la un perdonà l'altre. E quan foren en ço que's volgren departir, la un savi dix: - De la ventura que'ns és avenguda en la forest on venim, seguir-se-n'ha a nosaltres alcun profit. ¿Parria-us bo que, per la manera dels cinc arbres e per les deu condicions significades per lurs flors, cascun jorn una vegada, nos deputàssem,[+] e que seguíssem la manera que la dona d'Intel.ligència nos ha donada: e que tant de temps duràs nostra desputació tro que tots tres haguéssem una fe e una lig tan solament, e que enfre nós haguéssem manera d'honrar e servir la un L'altre, per ço que enans nos puscam concordar? Car guerra treball e mal-volença, e donar dan e honta, empatxa los hòmens a ésser concordants en una creença.-"

Ramon Llull
Libre del gentil e los tres savis (in finem) (+)

Introduction
The Rhetoric of the Dialogue

" . . . and here the three sages took leave of each other with great love and in a very agreeable way: each of them asked forgiveness of the others in case he might have proffered any unkind word against the religion of the other; and each of them did pardon the others. And when they were about to leave one of the sages said: Some profit should result from the venture that has happened to us in the forest. Would it not be good that, following the model of the five trees and the ten conditions represented by their flowers, we could discuss once every coming day the indications given to us by Dame Intelligence? Our discussions should continue as long as necessary until we arrive at one faith and one religion so that we will have a form of honoring each other and serving each other. This would be the quickest way to come to our mutual concord. For war, strained works and ill will produce harm and shame, hindering people in their efforts to reach an agreement on one belief."

Cf. Ramon Llull, *Obres essencials*, (+)
Barcelona (Editorial selecta), vol. I, 1957, p. 1138.

(+) Sic, sed legendum 'desputàssem'.

The chapters that follow do not elaborate a theory of the religious encounter. They are part of that very encounter. And it is out of this praxis that I would like to propose the following *attitudes* and *models* for the proper rhetoric in the meeting of religious traditions.

I do not elaborate now on the value of these attitudes or the merits of these models. This would require studying the function and nature of the metaphor as well as developing a theory of the religious encounter. I only describe some attitudes and models, although I will probably betray my sympathies in the form of critical considerations. The dialogue needs an adequate rhetoric—in the classical sense of the word.

1. Three Attitudes
a. Exclusivism

A believing member of a religion in one way or another considers his religion to be true. Now, the claim to truth has a certain built-in claim to exclusivity. If a given statement is true, its contradictory cannot also be true. And if a certain human tradition claims to offer a universal context for truth, anything contrary to that 'universal truth' will have to be declared false.

If, for instance, Islam embodies the true religion, a 'non-Islamic truth' cannot exist in the field of religion. Any long standing religious tradition, of course, will have developed the necessary distinctions so as not to appear too blunt. It will say, for instance, that there are degrees of truth and that any 'religious truth', if it is really true, 'is' already a Muslim one, although the people concerned may not be conscious of it. It will further distinguish an objective order of truth from a subjective one so that a person can be 'in good faith' and yet be in objective error, which as such will not be imputed against that person, etc.

This attitude has a certain element of heroism in it. You consecrate your life and dedicate your entire existence to something which is really worthy of being called a human cause, to something that claims to be not just a partial and imperfect truth, but a universal and even absolute truth. To be sure, an absolute God or Value has to be the final guarantee for such an attitude, so that you do not follow it because of personal whims or because you have uncritically raised your point of view to an absolute value. It is God's rights you defend when asserting your religion as 'absolute religion.' This does not imply an outright condemnation of the beliefs of all other human beings who have not received the 'grace' of your calling. You may consider this call a burden and a duty (to carry vicariously the responsibility for the whole world) more than as a privilege and a gift. Who are we to put conditions on the Almighty?

On the other hand, this attitude presents its difficulties. First, it carries with it the obvious danger of intolerance, hybris and contempt for others. "We belong to the club of turth." It further bears the intrinsic weakness of assuming an almost purely logical conception of truth and the uncritical attitude of an epistemological naiveté. Truth is many-faceted and even if you assume that God speaks an exclusive language, everything depends on your understanding of it so that you may never really know whether your interpretation is the *only* right one. To recur to a superhuman instance in the discussion among two religious beliefs does not solve any question, for it is often the case that God 'speaks' also to others, and both partners relying on God's authority will always need the human mediation, so that ultimately God's authority depends on Man's interpretation (of the divine revelation).

As a matter of fact, although there are many *de facto* remnants of an exclusivistic attitude today, it is hardly defended *de jure*. To use the Christian *skandalon*, for instance, to defend Christianity would amount to the very betrayal of that saying about the 'stumbling block'. It would be the height of hypocrisy to condemn others and justify oneself using the scandal of God's revelation as a rationale for defending one's own attitude: divine revelation ceases to be a scandal for you (for you seem to accept it without scandal)—and you hurl it at others.

b. Inclusivism

In the present world context one can hardly fail to discover positive and true values—even of the highest order—outside of one's own tradition. Traditional religions have to face this challenge. 'Splendid isolation' is no longer possible. The most plausible condition for the claim to truth of one's own tradition is to affirm at the same time that it includes at different levels all that there is of truth wherever it exists. The inclusivistic attitude will tend to reinterpret things in such a way as to make them not only palatable but also assimilable. Whenever facing a plain contradiction, for instance, it will make the necessary distinctions between different planes so as to be able to overcome that contradiction. It will tend to become a universalism of an existential or formal nature rather than of essential content. A doctrinal truth can hardly claim universality if it insists too much on specific contents because the grasping of the contents always implies a particular *'forma mentis'*. An attitude of tolerant admission of different planes will, on the contrary, have it easier. An umbrella pattern or a formal structure can easily embrace different thought-systems.

If Vedanta, for example, is really the end and acme of all the Vedas, these latter understood as the representation of all types of ultimate revelation, it can seemingly affirm that all sincere human affirmations have a place in its scheme because they represent different stages in the development of human consciousness and have a value in the particular context in which they are said. Nothing is rejected and all is fitted into its proper place.

This attitude has a certain quality of magnanimity and grandeur in it. You can follow your own path and do not need to condemn the other. You can even enter into communion with all other ways of life and, if you happen to have the real experience of inclusivity, you may be at peace not only with yourself, but with all other human and divine ways as well. You can be concrete in your allegiances and universal in your outlook.

On the other hand, this attitude also entails some difficulties. First, it also presents the danger of hybris, since it is only you who have the privilege of an all-embracing vision and tolerant attitude, you who allot to the others the place they must take in the universe. You are tolerant in your own eyes, but not in the eyes of those whose challenge your right to be on top. Furthermore it has the intrinsic difficulties of an almost alogical conception of truth and a built-in inner contradiction when the attitude is spelt out in theory and praxis.

If this attitude allows for a variegated expression of 'religious truth' so as to be able to include the most disparate systems of thought, it is bound to make of truth a purely relative. Truth here cannot have an independent intellectual content, for it is one thing for the parsi and another for the vaishnava, one thing for the atheist and another for the theist. So, it is also another thing for you—unless you jump outside the model because it is you who have the clue, you who find a place for all the different world views. But then your belief, conception, ideology, intuition or whatever name we may call it, becomes a supersystem the moment that you formulate it: you seem to understand the lower viewpoints and put them in their right places. You cannot avoid claiming for yourself a superior knowledge even if you deny that your conviction is another viewpoint. If you 'say', furthermore, that your position is only the ineffable fruit of a mystical insight, the moment that you put it into practice nothing prevents another from discovering and formulating the implicit assumptions of that attitude. Ultimately you claim to have a fuller truth in comparison with all the others who have only partial and relative truths.

As a matter of fact, although there are still many tendencies in several religious traditions that consider themselves all-inclusive, there are today only very few theoretical and philosophical formulations of a purely inclusivistic attitude. The claim of pluralism today is too strong to be so easily bypassed.

c. Parallelism

If your religion appears far from being perfect and yet it represents for you a symbol of the right path and a similar conviction seems to be the case for others, if you cannot dismiss the religious claim of the other nor assimilate it completely into your tradition, a plausible alternative is to assume that all are different creeds which, in spite of meanderings and crossings, actually run parallel to meet only in the ultimate, in the *eschaton*, at the very end of the human pilgrimage. Religions would then be parallel paths and our most urgent duty would be not to interfere with others, not to convert them or even to borrow from them, but to deepen our own respective traditions so that we may meet at the end, and in the depths of our own traditions. Be a better Christian, a better Marxist, a better Hindu and you will find unexpected riches and also points of contact with other people's ways.

This attitude presents very positive advantages. It is tolerant, it respects the others and does not judge them. It avoids muddy syncretisms and eclecticisms that concoct a religion according to our private tastes; it keeps the boundaries clear and spurs constant reform of one's own ways.

On the other hand, it too is not free of difficulties. First of all, it seems to go against the historical experience that the different religious and human traditions of the world have usually emerged from mutual interferences, influences and fertilizations. It too hastily assumes, furthermore, that every human tradition has in itself all the elements for further growth and development; in a word, it assumes the self-sufficiency of every tradition and seems to deny the need or convenience of mutual learning, or the need to walk outside the walls of one particular human tradition—as if in every one of them the entire human experience were crystallized or condensed. It flatters every one of us to hear that we possess *in nuce* all we need for a full human and religious maturity, but it splits the family of Man into watertight compartments, making any kind of conversion a real betrayal of one's own being. It allows growth, but not mutation. Even if we run parallel to each other, are there not *sangams, prayāgs*, affluents, inundations, natural and artificial dams, and above all, does not one and the same water flow 'heavenwards' in the veins of the human being? Mere parallelism eschews the real issues.

Notwithstanding, this attitude presents on the other hand more prospects for an initial working hypothesis today. It carries a note of hope and patience at the same time; hope that we will meet at the end and patience that meanwhile we have to bear our differences. Yet when facing concrete problems of interferences, mutual influences and even dialogue one cannot just wait until this *kalpa* comes to an end or the *eschaton* appears. All crossings are dangerous, but there is no new life without *maithuna*.

* * * * *

I have described these three attitudes as an example of basic postures which when put to work becomes, of course, much more sophisticated. When the encounter actually takes place, be it in actual facts or in the more conscious dialogue, one needs some root-metaphors in order to articulate the different problems. It is here that some models may prove useful. I shall briefly describe three of them.

2.-Three Models

a. The Physical Model: The Rainbow

The different religious traditions of mankind are like the almost infinite number of colors that appear once the divine or simply white light of reality falls on the prism of human experience: it diffracts into innumerable traditions, doctrines and religions. Green is not yellow, Hinduism is not Buddhism and yet at the fringes one cannot know, except by postulating it artificially, where yellow ends and green begins. Even more, through any particular color, viz. religion, one can reach the source of the white light. Any follower of a human tradition is given the possibility of reaching his or her destination, fullness, salvation provided there is a beam of light and not sheer darkness. If two colors mix, they may sire another. Similarly with religious traditions, the meeting of two may give birth to a new one. In point of fact, most of the known religions today are results of such mutual fecundations (Aryans-dravidians, Jews-Greeks, Indians-Muslims, etc.). Further, it is only from an agreed point of view that we can judge a religion over against another. Regarding social concern, for instance, one tradition may be more fruitful than another, but the latter may be more powerful than the former in securing personal happiness. We may begin the rainbow with the infra-red, or with the ultra-violet, or choose, for instance, 5.000 Angstroms as the central point, etc. Furthermore, within the green area all will appear under that particular light. A similar object within the red area will look reddish. This model reminds us that the context is paramount in comparing 'religious truths.' Nor is this all. Just as the color of a body is the only color generally not absorbed by that body, this model would remind us also that a religion similarly absorbs all other colors and hides them in its bosom, so that its external color is in truth only its appearance, its message to the outer world, but not the totality of its nature. We come to this realization when we attempt to understand a religion from within. The real body that has received the entire beam of white light keeps for itself all the other colors so that it would not accord with truth to judge a religion only from its outer color. This metaphor can still take more refinements. One particular religion may include only a few beams of light while another may cover a wider aspect of the spectrum. Time and space may (like the principle of Doppler-

Fizeau) introduce modifications in the wave-length of a particular tradition, so that it changes down the ages or along with the places. What is a Christian in the India of the twentieth century may be far different from what was considered such in tenth century France.

This metaphor does not necessarily imply that all the religions are the same, that there may not be black or colorless spots, that for some particular problems only one particular color may be the appropriate one, etc. The metaphor, moreover, could still serve to contest the right of something which does not have light in it to be called a religious tradition. A humanistic critique of traditional religions, for instance, may well call obscurantistic all the religions of the past and deny to them the character of bearing light; only the enlightenment traditions of rationalism, marxism and humanism, let us say, would come into consideration. I am citing this extreme case in order to clarify the immense variation possible in the use of this root-metaphor. It could even provide an image for the conception of one particular religion considering itself as the white beam and all the others refractions of that primordial religiousness. Or, on the contrary, it may offer an example of how to say that the variety of religions belongs to the beauty and richness of the human situation: since it is only the entire rainbow that provides a complete picture of the true religious dimension of Man.

Yet the value of a model comes not only from its possible applicability, but also from its connaturality with the phenomenon under analysis. The physical fact of the rainbow in this case helps us to explain the intricacies of the anthropological phenomenon of religion.

b. The Geometrical Model: The Topological Invariant

If in the first model diffraction is what produces the different lights, viz. religions, transformation is the cause of the different forms and shapes of geometrical figures, viz. of religions, in our second model.

In and through space and also due to the influence of

time, a primordial and original form takes on an almost indefi-
nite number of possible transformations through the twisting
of Men, the stretching by history, the bending by natural
forces and so on. Religions appear different and even mutually
irreconcilable until or unless a topological invariant is found.
This invariant does not need to be a single one for all religions.
Some may prefer to hold the theory of families of religions,
while others may try to work out the hypothesis that all the
different human ways come from a fundamental experience
transformed according to laws, which as in any geometrical
case have first to be discovered. Or again, others may say that
religions are actually different until the corresponding topological transformations have been constructed. The model
is polyvalent. Homeomorphism is not the same as analogy: it
represents a functional equivalence discovered through a topological transformation. Brahman and God are not merely
two analogous names; they are homeomorphic in the sense
that each of them stands for something that performs an
equivalent function within their respective systems. But this
can only be formulated once the homeomorphism of a topological equivalence has been found. Religions which may
appear at first sight very different from each other may find
their connections once the topological transformation is discovered that permits connecting the two traditions under
consideration. This model offers a challenge to further study
and prevents us from drawing hurried conclusions. A literal
use of the topological model would assume not only that all
religions are transformations of a primordial experience, intuition or datum (as would be the case with the Rainbow model),
but also that each religious tradition is a dimension of the
other, that there is a kind of 'circumincessio' or 'perichoresis'
or 'pratītyasamutpāda' among all the religious traditions of the
world so that mere contiguity models are insufficient to express their relation. Religions do not stand side by side, but
they are actually intertwined and inside each other. Vishnu
dwells in the heart of Shiva and vice-versa. Each religion
represents the whole for that particular human group and in a

certain way 'is' the religion of the other group only in a different topoligical form. Perhaps this may be too optimistic a view, but the model provides also for the necessary cautions or restrictions. One cannot a priori, for instance, formulate this theory, but it may well be a working hypothesis spurring our minds towards some transcendental unity of the religious experience of Man. It is clear that this model does not exclude a divine factor nor a critical evaluation of the human traditions. Sometimes it may be that we do not succeed in finding the corresponding topological equivalence, but sometimes it may also be that such a transformation does not exist.

The comparison among religions according to this model would then not be the business of finding analogies, which are bound to be always somewhat superficial and need a *primum analogatum* as point of reference (which should already belong to the traditions compared if the comparison is to be fair), but would rather be the business of understanding religions from within and discovering their concrete structures, and of finding out their corresponding homeomorphisms. Religious variety would appear here not so much a bountifully colorful universe as different appearances of an inner structure detectable only in a deeper intuition, be this called mystical or scientific.

Now, the topological laws do not need to be merely of a rational or logical nature, as is the case with geometrical topology. They could as well be historical or *sui generis*. In a word, the topological model is not only useful for possible doctrinal equivalents; it could also serve to explore other forms of correspondence and equivalence. We may succeed in explaining, for instance, how primitive Buddhism was reabsorbed in India through a certain advaita by means of finding the proper topological laws of transformation.

c. The Anthropological Model: Language

Whatever theory we may defend regarding the origin and nature of religion, whether it be a divine gift or a human invention or both, the fact remains that it is at least a human reality and as such coextensive with another also at least human reality called language. This model considers each religion as a language. This model has ancient antecedents. To the widespread old belief that there were seventy-two languages, some added the conviction that there were equally seventy-two religions. "Item dixit—say the proceedings of an inquisitorial process of the XIII century in Bologna, condemning a Cathar—, quod sicut sunt LXII lingue, ita sunt LXII fides."

Any religion is complete as any language is also capable of expressing everything that it feels the need to express. Any religion is open to growth and evolution as any language is. Both are capable of expressing or adopting new shades of meaning, of shifting idioms or emphases, refining ways of expression and changing them. When a new need is felt in any religious or linguistic world, there are always means of dealing with that need. Furthermore, although any language is a world in itself, it is not without relations with neighboring languages, borrowing from them and open to mutual influences. And yet each language only takes as much as it can assimilate from a foreign language. Similarly with religions: they influence each other and borrow from one another without losing their identity. As an extreme case a religion, like a language, may disappear entirely. And the reasons also seem very similar— conquest, decadence, emigration, etc.

From the internal point of view of each language and religion, it makes little sense to say that one language is more perfect that another, for you can in your language (as well as in your religion) say all that you feel you need to say. If you would feel the need to say something else or something different, you would say it. If you use only one word for camel and hundreds for the different metals, and another language does just the opposite, it is because you have different patterns of differentiation for camels and metals. It is the same with religions. You may have only one word for wisdom, God, compassion or virtue and another religion scores of them.

The great problem appears when we come to the encounter

of languages—and religions. The question here is translation. Religions are equivalent to the same extent that languages are translatable, and they are unique as much as languages are untranslatable. There is the common world of objectifiable objects. They are the objects of empirical or logical verification. This is the realm of terms. Each term is an epistemic sign standing for an empirically or logically verifiable object. The terms 'tree', 'wine', 'atom', 'four', can be translated into any given language if we have a method of empirically pointing out a visible thing (tree), a physically recognizable substance (wine), a physico-mathematically definable entity (atom) and a logical cipher (four). Each of these cases demands some specific conditions, but we may assume that these conditions can all be empirically or logically verifiable once a certain axiom is accepted. In short, all terms are translatable insofar as a name could easily be invented or adopted even by a language which might lack a particular term ('atom' for instance). Similarly, all religions have a translatable sphere: all refer to the human being, to his well-being, to overcoming the possible obstacles to it, and the like. Religious terms—qua terms—are translatable.

The most important part of a language as well as of a religion, however, is not terms but words, i.e., not epistemic signs to orient us in the world of objects, but living symbols to allow us to live in the world of Men and Gods. Now, words are not objectifiable. A word is not totally separable from the meaning we give to it and each of us in fact gives different shades of meaning to the same word. A word reflects a total human experience and cannot be severed from it. A word is not empirically or logically detectable. When we say 'justice,' 'dharma,' 'karunā,' we cannot point to an object, but have to refer to crystallizations of human experiences that vary with people, places, ages, etc. We cannot properly speaking translate words. We can only transplant them along with a certain surrounding context which gives them meaning and offers the horizon over against which they can be understood, i.e., assimilated within another horizon. And even then the transplanted word, if it survives, will soon extend its roots in the soil and acquire new aspects, connotations, etc. Similarly with religions: they are not translatable like terms; only certain transplants are possible under appropriate conditions. There is not an object 'God,' 'justice,' or 'Brahman,' a thing in itself independent of those living words, over against which we may check the correction of the translation. In order to translate them we have to transplant the corresponding world view that makes those words say what they intend to say. A non-saying word is like a non-sung song. If the word is not heard as saying what it intends to say, we have not actually translated that word. The translation of religious insights cannot be done unless the insight that has originated that word is also transplanted. Now for this, a mere 'sight' from the outside is not sufficient. We may then translate only the outer carcass of a word and not its real meaning. No word can be cut from its speaker if it has to remain an authentic word and not a mere term. The translator has to be also a speaker in that foreign language, in that alien tradition; he has to be a true spokesman for that religion; he has to be, to a certain extent (that I shall not describe further here), convinced of the truth he conveys, converted to the tradition from which he translates. Here I am already in the intra-religious dialogue.

The translator has to speak the 'foreign' language as his own. As long as we speak a language translating from another, we shall never speak fluently or even correctly. Only when we speak that language, only when you 'speak' that religion as your own will you really be able to be a spokesman for it, a genuine translator. And this obviously implies at the same time that you have not forgotten your native tongue, that you are equally capable of expressing yourself in the other linguistic world. It is then that one begins to wonder at the exactness of the translations, or as the expression still goes, at the 'fidelity' of many a translation. Are you keeping fidelity to both Brahman and God, dharma and religion (or justice, or order?) when you translate in that way? Or are you obliged to enlarge, to deepen and to stretch your own language in order to make place for the insights of the other? And this may be the case even with terms that are in part empirically verifiable. Are you so sure that when you translate *gau* with 'cow' you are not misleading the modern English reader is you let him believe that you speak merely of a bovine female related perhaps to cowboys but not to the *kāmadhenu? Gau* is more than a zoological name as *sūrya* (sun) is more than a mere name for an astronomical or physical body.

The linguistic model helps also in the complicated problem of Comparative Religion. Only when we have a common language can we begin to compare, i.e., to weigh against a common background. Only then may a mutual understanding take place. This model, moreover, makes it clear that we cannot compare languages (religions) outside language (religion) and that there is no language (religion) except in concrete languages (religions). Comparative religion can only be comparative religions from the standpoint of the concrete religions themselves. This demands an entirely new method from that arising out of the assumption that there is a non-religious neutral 'reason' entitled to pass comparative judgments in the field of religions.

3. Pluralism

The mention of pluralism by way of conclusion may not be out of place. The aim of the intrareligious dialogue is understanding. It is not to win over the other or to come to a total agreement or a universal religion. The ideal is communication in order to bridge the gulfs of mutual ignorance and misunderstandings between the different cultures of the world, letting them speak and speak out their own insights in their own languages. Some may wish even to reach communion, but this does not imply at all that the aim is a uniform unity or a reduction of all the pluralistic variety of Man into one single religion, system, ideology or tradition. Pluralism stands between unrelated plurality and a monolithic unity. It implies that the human condition in its present reality should not be neglected, let alone despised in favor of an ideal (?) situation of human uniformity. On the contrary, it takes our factual situation as real and affirms that in the actual polarities of our human existence we find our real being.

Varanasi,
February, Vasantpancamī, 1978

I. FAITH AND BELIEF
A Multireligious Experience

te 'pi mām eva, . . . yajanti
Me they also worship.

BG IX, 23

Whoever wishes to care for me,
let him look after the sick ones.

Vinayapiṭaka I, 302

ἐμοὶ ἐποιήϐατε
mihi fecistis
you did it unto me.

Mt. 25:40

1. INTRODUCTION

The distinction between faith and belief, along with the thesis that faith is a constitutive human dimension, represents more than just an intellectual venture. It is equally an existential adventure: a human pilgrimage within religious traditions divided by multisecular walls of history, philosophies, theologies and prejudices. It has been my *karma* to undergo such experiences without artificially or even reflectively preparing them. A decade ago, after fifteen years' absence from the European literary scene, the plainest and yet the most searching question to ask me was: How have I fared? And although my human pilgrimage was not yet finished, I used to give a straightforward—obviously incomplete—answer: I 'left' as a Christian, I 'found' myself a Hindu and I 'return' a Buddhist, without having ceased to be a Christian. Some people nevertheless wonder whether such an attitude is objectively tenable or even intelligible. Here is a reply in outline that I hope will also throw some light on the spiritual condition of humankind today—even if it belongs to my historical past.

2. ECUMENISM TODAY

In ancient Greece, *oikumene* referred to household management. When the domestic sense broadened the word came to mean the world, but still within a rather narrow compass— just as when someone says 'everybody' has left Madrid for their August vacation, although the only water most of the

2

people ever see is the trickle in their own channelled River Manzanares. Our age prides itself on its ecumenical spirit and has indeed risen above the clan mentality far enough to acknowledge the right of other clans to exist, whether they call themselves philosophical systems, religious beliefs, races or nations. But for all their importance, these ecumenisms generally remain very restricted, still far removed from an *ecumenical ecumenism* that means more than the mere notion that people everywhere are human, or that my own views and judgments can be exported quite safely to other countries.

The great temptation for ecumenism is to extrapolate—to use a native growth beyond the bounds of its native soil. We have seen what comes of exporting European and American democracy; we know that the baffling population explosion over much of the world's surface comes of exporting antibiotics, DDT and the like. No one-way movement—certainly not exporting a Gospel—can solve our present problems. I do not for a moment suggest that there be no crossing of borders. I am only saying that most solutions to our problems remain terribly provincial; we do not yet have categories adequate to the exigencies of our *kairos*.

3. THE PROVINCE AND THE PARISH

The confrontation of religions provides an instructive instance of what I am trying to say. Men construct a philosophy or theology of religion and consider it universal. To be more precise, they dash off Judeo-Graeco-Modern categories and with these attempt to lay hold of religious, cultural and philosophical phenomena lying many a mile beyond the remotest colony (as it is called), the farthest outpost of their *oikumene*. Thus Asia, for example, compelled to speak in some European language, will have to say 'way' instead of *tao*, 'God' instead of *Brahman* and 'soul' instead of *ātman*; it must translate *dharma* as 'justice', *chan* as 'meditation', and so forth. But the problem lies even deeper than the difficulty of suitably translating ideas belonging to other cultural contexts. The problem cannot be 'computerized', so to speak, because it involves the very laws that govern the working of our minds—and of computers to boot.

This 'neocolonialistic' situation prompts me to observe that while the *province* may betoken narrowness of mind bordering on myopia and lead to fanaticism and intolerance, the *parish* might connote safeguarding a particular reality, a human scale of things, organic and personal life. The parish is by its very nature a miniature universe quantitatively speaking, but the entire universe speaking qualitatively (although symbolically). Nevertheless, from the steeple of the parish church many other steeples can be seen. A theological hermeneutic of this symbol tells us that the parish will be whole only when the Pantocrator, the Lord of all the universe, is at its center and there holds communion (this is the right word) with the whole world. Wisdom reaches its pinnacle in a happy commingling of universal and concrete, intellectual and vital, masculine and feminine, divine and human—in short, in cosmotheandric experience. 'Ecumenical ecumenism', a phrase I diffidently put forward some years ago and that now seems to be sweeping the board, might well express this blend of household hearth and universal humanness. The parish lived in all its depth and scope stands for the same thing: homey, down-to-earth, regional things; it means dialect, personal roots, personalizing forms and at the same time an awareness that we all draw nourishment from a common sap, that one sky arches over us all, that a single mother earth sustains us all.[1] Ecumenical ecumenism does not mean cloudy universalism or indiscriminate syncretism; nor a narrow, crude particularism or barren, fanatical individualism. Instead it attempts a happy blending—which I would make bold to call androgynous before calling it theandric—of these two poles, the universal and the concrete, which set up the tension in every creature. In other words, the identity our age so frantically seeks is not individuality (which ends in solipsism), nor generality (which ends in alienation), but the awareness of that constitutive relativity which makes of us but connections in the mysterious warp and woof of being. But I should not go on cheering *pro domo mea* when I am saying my house is the cottage of mankind.

4. AN OBJECTIFIED AUTOBIOGRAPHICAL FRAGMENT

Before embarking on a clearer, more scholarly treatment of the subject, I should like to present it in a personal way, psychological if you will—although not strictly autobiographical.

Here I am a Man brought up in the strictest orthodoxy, who has lived as well in a milieu that is 'microdox' from every point of view. It will not do to say now that if I managed to survive it was thanks to seeds of true life sown even before I had reached the age of reason. This Man goes forth, forsaking the land of Ur, to dwell in the land of Men (indeed he knew it before, but not through experience, not in his flesh like Job). Instantly he finds himself confronted by a dilemma: Either he must condemn everything around him as error and sin, or he must throw overboard the exclusivistic and monopolistic notions he has been told embody truth—truth that must be simple and unique, revealed once and for all, that speaks through infallible organs, and so on. None of the answers people reply to this dilemma satisfy him. The eclectic answer flouts logic and sometimes common sense as well. He cannot make do with the 'orthodox' answer that merely concocts casuistic shifts so that some nook is left for those who profess error through no fault of their own: It does not convince him either as a whole or in its details. So he overcomes the temptation of *relativism* by acknowledging *relativity*. Instead of everything falling into an agnostic or indifferent relativism, everything is wrapped in an utter relativity of radical interdependence because every being is a function in the hierarchical order of beings and has its own place in the dynamism of history, a place not incidental to the thing but actually making the thing what it is.

But the personal problem went deeper still. It involved

more than rising above provincialism or acknowledging that today philosophy must recognize cultural differences and account for Man's pluralism. One had to safeguard the parish, uphold one's identity, live by one's faith and yet not cut oneself from Men, not look on oneself as a special, privileged being. Can a Man keep his feet firmly planted on the ground—on his native soil—while his arms embrace the most distant heavens? Indeed, the problem was trying to live one's faith without an exclusivity that appears outrageously unjust and false even when decked out in notions of grace, election or what have you. In other words, the whole idea of belonging to a chosen people, of practicing the true religion, of being a privileged creature, struck me not as a grace but a disgrace. Not that I felt myself unworthy, but I thought it would ill become me to discriminate in such a fashion and I thought it would ill become God to do so. I am well aware of the innumerable theoretical ways to get around the objection. I do not claim this idea runs counter to God's goodness or justice, which presumably is not affected by our revulsion; I contend only that this idea contravenes the freedom and joy I would look for in a belief that enables the human being to grow to full stature. It is not as though the conception of God could not outride such objections; it is rather that such a conception of God reflects little credit on the Man who thinks it up. I share, if you like, the well-known outlook of the *Bodhisattva* who forestalls his own beatitude until the last Man has attained it; or of Moses and Paul who would rather be stricken from the Book of Life than saved alone. In short, can one live a religious faith to the full without being cut off from Men either quantitatively or qualitatively—either from the whole of mankind down the ages or from whatever is human in them and in oneself?

5. UNIVERSALITY AND CONCRETENESS

The problem comes down to this: Can one lead a universal life in the concrete? Is it feasible to live by faith that is at once embodied—incarnational—and transcendent? Is the concrete incompatible with the universal, the categorical with the transcendental?

But here we have only the first part of the problem. The second part emerges when we must contend with people holding different views who claim the right to argue just as we do and to draw conclusions in favor of their own views. After all, the rules must be the same for both sides; I may embrace my neighbor only if I let him embrace me at the same time; I may universalize my belief and reform my religion only if, at the same time, I let my neighbor do the same with his. Taking this attitude, am I not endangering an entire conception of truth based on the principle of property?

But once our seven-league boots have swept us to the pinnacle of the problem, it is best to start down again along one particular path, to try to shed light on a single facet of the problem and afterwards cite an example to corroborate our words.[2] The aspect I would like to rough out may be focused in the distinction already made between faith and belief.[3]

6. THE ENCOUNTER OF BELIEFS

Let us return to our point of departure and say that I (who for the present purposes can be anybody) live by certain underlying persuasions that express themselves in my personal act of faith: I believe in a God who made the universe, in a Christ who redeemed mankind, in a Spirit who is our pledge of everlasting life and so forth. For me all these phrases are just translations into a given language understandable in a given tradition, of something that outsoars all utterance. I refer to those dogmas (as they are called) which make sense of my life and convey what truth is for me. I cannot dispense with these phrases because they make up my belief; but neither must I forget that they are phrases, neither more nor less.

On this level I encounter a person who belongs to another religious tradition. He tells me he does not believe in God, he has no idea who Christ is and he thinks there is no life but the present one we all experience. He may tell me further that he believes in Buddha as an Enlightened One who has pointed out the road to salvation, and that salvation consists in blotting out all existence.

The first requisite for dialogue is that we understand each other. The first prerequisite for this understanding on the intellectual level is that we speak the same language, lest we use different words to convey the same idea and therefore take them to mean different things. Now in order to know we speak the same language we need a lodestar somewhere outside the framework of language: We must be able to point with the finger of the mind, or some other sign, to the 'thing' when we use the same or different words.

Let us assume (which is assuming a great deal, but so we must if we are to make any headway) we have reached agreement about our language and we are using words to signify ideas defined sharply enough to make discussion possible.

The exchange might then take some such form: 'I believe in God as embodying the truth that makes sense of my life and the things around me.' 'I, on the other hand, believe in the nonexistence of such a being and this nonexistence is precisely what enables me to believe in the truth of things, and to make sense of my life and the things around me.' Here one person makes 'God' the keystone of his existence, salvation, etc., while the other makes his conviction of 'no God' the keystone of the same thing. More simply put: The first declares 'God is the truth', the second says, 'no-God is the truth'.

Both believe in truth, but the phrase 'God exists' sums up the truth for one Man, while for the other the phrase 'God does not exist' sums it up. At this point the more exact statement enters: Both have *faith* in the truth, but for the one this faith expresses itself in the *belief* that 'God exists', while for the other it expresses itself in the contrary proposition, 'God does not exist'.

If one said 'truth exists' and the other, 'truth does not exist', then *faith* would be grounded in each one's conviction of what his own proposition means, and *belief* would be the conviction set forth in each one's proposition. Even to bluntly refuse any dialogue implies the faith that one possesses the truth and the belief that the formula cannot be sundered from the thing formulated. Affirming absurdity or postulating nothingness can be *beliefs* of the same *faith* that moves others to believe in God or in Man.

7. KRSNA AND CHRIST

Here, by acknowledging that a single faith may express itself in contrasting and even contradictory beliefs, dialogue would start. The next step is to understand the other's position, and at once a tremendous difficulty arises. I can never understand his position as he does—and this is the only real understanding between people—unless I share his view; in a word, unless I judge it to be somewhat true. It is contradictory to imagine I understand another's view when at the same time I call it false. I may indeed say I understand my partner in dialogue better than he understands himself. I may say he is mistaken because he contradicts himself, even say I understand his position because I understand his premises; but clearly I cannot uphold his view as he does unless I share it. When I say I understand a proposition and consider it untrue, in the first place I do not understand it because, by definition, truth alone is intelligible (if I understand a thing I always understand it *sub ratione veritatis*); in the second place I certainly do not understand it in the way of someone who holds it to be true. Accordingly, to understand is to be converted to the truth one understands.[4]

Now the problem becomes even more involved. Let us consider an example: My partner declares that one arrives at salvation through Krsna, the supreme epiphany of the Godhead. If I understand *what* he is saying I must simply yield my assent, as he does his, to the truth of that declaration. That is, I share his point of view—even though I may still believe that mine may be subtler and may in fact incorporate his. Otherwise I must say I do not understand *it,* or withdraw intelligibility to an earlier level: I understand *him*, I know what he *means* because I understand that his declaration follows from a series of assumptions that lead him to believe what he says; but I do not share his belief in the truth of those assump-

tions. Then the problem comes down to understanding these
assumptions and their intelligibility. Hence dialogue serves
the useful purpose of laying bare our own assumptions and
those of others, thereby giving us a more critically grounded
conviction of what we hold to be true.

To my mind the most far-reaching conclusions follow
from what has been said up to this point, but I have yet a good
deal more to say. The real religious or theological task, if you
will, begins when the two views meet head-on inside oneself,
when dialogue prompts genuine religious pondering, and
even a religious crisis, at the bottom of a Man's heart; when
interpersonal dialogue turns into intrapersonal soliloquy.

Let us suppose I have grasped the basic belief of a Vaiṣṇava and therefore share it; in other words I can honestly
affirm what an orthodox Vaiṣṇava believes. Does this mean I
have deserted my original religious position? Are the two
beliefs not essentially irreconcilable? Either I believe in Kṛṣṇa
or I believe in Christ. Either I am a Christian and declare Jesus
as the Savior of mankind, or I follow Kṛṣṇa and acknowledge
him as the true Savior of mankind. Is it not a double betrayal to
try to reconcile these two beliefs, which conflict at every
point? Can we find any way out of this dilemma?

At this juncture, the dialogue of which I speak emerges
not as a mere academic device or an intellectual amusement,
but a spiritual matter of the first rank, a religious act that itself
engages faith, hope and love. Dialogue is not bare methodology but an essential part of the religious act par excellence:
loving God above all things and one's neighbor as oneself. If
we believe that our neighbor lies entangled in falsehood and
superstition we can hardly love him as ourselves, without a
hypocritical, pitying love that moves us to try plucking the
mote out of his eye. Love for our neighbor also makes intellectual demands. For as the Christian tradition has said over
and over again, you cannot love your neighbor as yourself
without loving God. Perhaps I can love the other person as
other which means as an object to me (as useful, pleasant, kind,
beautiful, complementary to me, something of this sort); but I

cannot love him as *myself* unless I take my place on the one bit of higher ground that will hold us both—unless I love God. God is the unique locus where my selfhood and my neighbor's coincide, consequently the one place that enables me to love him as he loves his own self without any attempt at molding him.[5]

For this very reason I cannot love God unless I love my neighbor, because God is that transcending of my 'I' that puts me in touch with my neighbor. Saint Augustine (could we expect otherwise?) says so word for word: 'Because a Man loves his neighbor as himself only if he loves God *(Diligit enim unusquisque proximum suum tamquam seipsum, si diligit Deum)*'. Understanding my neighbor means understanding him as he understands himself, which can be done only if I rise above the subject-object dichotomy, cease to know him as an object and come to know him as myself. Only if there exists a Self in which we communicate does it become possible to know and love another as Oneself. Anyone with half an eye can see what follows and how it upsets the false privacy in which we are inclined to shut ourselves away. True intimacy does not stiffen or deaden us, because within that Self (God is not the Other, he is the One) dwell life, dialogue and love. This is in fact the Trinitarian mystery, but we must not wander from our present topic.

Let no one object that the Gospel commission is not to dialogue with all nations but to go and teach them—in the first place, because here we are not conducting apologetics of any sort and so feel under no obligation to prove the orthodoxy of any view; and in the second place because that commission is cited in a mutilated form and altogether out of context. The complete text makes it quite clear that the 'discipleship' it refers to consists precisely in serving one's fellows and loving them, and they are not served if I am the one who lays down how the master is to be served. Moreover, the commission is purely charismatic, it calls for the power to work miracles. Who would like to throw the first stone?

Be that as it may, no one can fail to see the religious

challenge of the situation I have set forth. A really devout
mind will ask how we can embrace the faith of our neighbor
without going astray in our own. Indeed how can we embrace
it at all? Can my faith absorb another's belief? Here I think we
have the touchstone for any genuine life of faith in our day: We
must believe those who do not believe, just as we must love
those who do not love.

8. THE MULTIRELIGIOUS EXPERIENCE

Now I should like to sketch the religious attitude of a
Man embarked on such a venture. He starts by making a real,
heartfelt, unselfish effort—a bold and hazardous one—to
understand the belief, the world, the archetypes, the culture,
the mythical and conceptual background, the emotional and
historical associations of his fellows from the inside. In short,
he seriously attempts an existential incarnation of himself into
another world—which obviously involves prayer, initiation,
study and worship. He does this not by way of trial but rather
with a spirit of faith in a truth that transcends us and a goodness
that upholds us when we truly love our neighbor—which does
not mean, as I have said, eliminating the intellect from this
enterprise. It is not experimentation but a genuine experience
undergone within one's own faith. Consequently that experience is forbidden, or rather does not become possible, unless
he has established in himself the distinction between his faith
(ever transcendent, unutterable and open) and his belief (an
intellectual, emotional and cultural embodiment of that faith
within the framework of a particular tradition that, yes, demands his loyalty, but not that he betray the rest of mankind). I
need hardly add that not everyone is called to such an under-
taking, nor is everyone capable of it. Besides a particular cast
of mind, it presupposes perhaps a special constellation in one's
character and background that enables one to undergo the
experience without any taint of exoticism, exhibitionism or
simply unremitting intellectualism. In a word, a Man needs a
kind of connaturality to go through that venture in a genuine
way. I repeat: It does not mean experimenting either with

one's own faith or with that of others. Faith can only be lived, but living it may at times demand risking it in order to remain faithful.

Moreover, this risk of faith must be understood as emerging from one's own faith itself; not from doubting what one believes, but deepening and enriching it. This risk should not be understood as an intellectual or religious curiosity but as a dynamic of faith itself, which discloses another religious world in one's neighbor that we can neither ignore nor brush aside, but must try to take up, integrate into our own. What is more, when faith claims universality, the faith of the neighbor automatically becomes a problem that cannot be evaded.

Abstract principles do not enable a Man to foresee what will happen in such an encounter; he must be prepared to stake everything he is and believes, not because he harbors doubts about it, nor yet because he says at the back of his mind that he is conducting some sort of methodological *epoché* (which at this juncture in history would be unnatural and unthinkable[6]), but because the venture hazards—or to be more precise, let us say makes possible—a conversion so thoroughgoing that the convictions and beliefs he had hitherto held may vanish or undergo a far-reaching change. Unquestionably the venture is perilous; you gamble your life. Hardly anyone would be equal to it but for the very drive of faith that invites us to hazard our life without fear, even to lose it.

9. INTERPRETING THE EXPERIENCE

Only afterwards can we describe what happens. I shall attempt to do this in the space of a few paragraphs.

Man can live only by truth; falsehood offers the mind no nourishment.[7] If my partner believes in Kṛṣṇa it is because he believes Kṛṣṇa embodies truth and this belief enters into the very truth of what he believes. I can understand this only if I also believe in the truth he believes, perhaps under rather a different guise. Whatever can be said of objective truth, religious belief is a highly personal and so subjective thing; the faith that saves is always personal and subjective. The Kṛṣṇa of our dialogue is not a historical or mythological figure but the Kṛṣṇa of faith, of my interlocutor's personal faith. His belief is the one I must assume, sharing his truth, the truth of the Kṛṣṇa of faith.

My own faith must be strong enough for me to do this— open and deep enough to work its way into the Vaiṣṇava world and share that world's ups and downs. First of all, my faith must be naked enough to be clothed in all those forms with no misgivings about slipping into heresy or apostasy. (Anyone who *thinks* he will be betraying his faith should not and cannot embark on this venture.) Then, in a second moment, my intrareligious soliloquy will have to blend my earlier beliefs with those acquired later, according to my lights and con- science (this entire procedure, of course, is also valid for my partner).

My partner in dialogue will then judge whether what I have learned of Kṛṣṇa is sound or not. I will have to give him an account of my belief and he will tell me whether what I say about Kṛṣṇa—one of the epiphanies of God and his love for Men, eminently one of God's names, a real symbol of the freedom of God and so forth—represents fundamental belief in Kṛṣṇa or not.

Once this first step has been taken, I must next explain to myself, and also to my interlocutor, how I blend this new religious experience of mine with belief in Christ.

Here an alternative lies before me: Either I have ceased to be a Christian—belief in Kṛṣṇa has supplanted my belief in Christ, I have found a loftier, fuller divine reality in Kṛṣṇa than in Christ—or else I am able to establish a special kind of bond between the two that both religions, or at least one of them, *can* acknowledge and accept (I do not say they already *have* accepted it).

If the specific problem is talked over not only with the uninvolvement befitting investigators into religion but also on a spiritual level high enough to rule out what may be called fundamentalist microdoxy, then we could in most cases reach a solution where each tradition finds the other's reading of it valid, therefore at least partially orthodox. I say 'partially' because each belief is integrated into a wider whole, which does not need to be accepted by the other party.

This example brings in a set of propositions that may answer the requirements of orthodoxy on both sides. With regard to traditional Christianity I would say: The unutterable, transcendent, everlasting God has never left Men without witness to himself and has always wisely looked after his creatures. That one mystery at work since the dawn of time, whose delight is to be with the children of Men, has disclosed to them God's kindness, the godliness of love, the gladness of living, the nature of worship and a set of rites with which to give their earthly existence meaning. That same mystery, hidden away for aeons, unveils itself in Christ in the last days with a special historical consciousness, so that the incorporation of the peoples into the *historical* dynamism of the world entails a certain relationship with Christ.

What may trouble the Christian mind about this sketch is the nature of the relationship between Christ and Kṛṣṇa. I shall make no attempt to deal with this problem at present. It is enough to say, first, that the difficulty strikes me as Graeco-Western, or rather philosophical, more than strictly Christian; second, that the identity need not be one of personal substance—a functional identity will do. I am not evading the problem; I merely point out its parameters. Perhaps mythic terms best serve to intimate the connection between Christ and Kṛṣṇa, but obviously the connection is something other than flat identity. I mean there is no need to say Christ is Kṛṣṇa, or the one a foreshadowing or fulfillment of the other in order to indicate their special relationship. At this point we feel the lack of a theology dealing with the encounter between religions. The problem of the one and the many also crops up here, albeit in a new form. But the place of Vaiṣṇavism in the Christian economy of salvation might very well be found here, within the framework of a universal economy of salvation and in a certain mysterious presence of the Lord in a multitude of epiphanies.

Something parallel could be said from the Vaiṣṇava side. We do not propose to argue whether the theology of Kṛṣṇa is the most perfect there is, blending the human element in its fullness with the godly one within the strictest demands of the Absolute. What may trouble the Vaiṣṇava mind is the peculiar emphasis laid upon historicity, perhaps to the detriment of an ever-original and genuine religious experience that does not need to rely on the faith of others, but discovers by itself the living symbol of belief. What may further bother a devotee of Kṛṣṇa is what he feels to be the Christian reductionism of religion to morals and of Christ to a single man. Perhaps Christians could answer and the dialogue could go on, but we merely wish to show that belief in Kṛṣṇa need not rule out acknowledging Jesus as an epiphany of God at one particular moment in history.

The basic issue for discussion would be the ultimate nature of the two divine epiphanies. While the Christian will say that Christ is the fullness and apex of God's every *epiphany*, the Vaiṣṇava will be moved to say that nothing can outdo the *theophany* of Kṛṣṇa. Nevertheless the difficulty can be overcome by mutual understanding. In terms of belonging to one or the other religious body (according to traditional standard, although nothing can halt the growth of tradition), the difficulty is for the time being insuperable; but we are now talking about something else, about dialogue that *is* true dialogue and therefore brings each side to understand and share the basic attitude of the other. Here the difficulty is not insuperable because, in the first place, when the matter is raised in this down-to-earth, existential way one may perfectly well say that the heart of the matter is not deciding who holds the 'objective' primacy, since by living in accordance with their particular persuasions and beliefs both will attain to what they sincerely believe; in the second place, because the question of Christ and Kṛṣṇa is not a speculation outside time and so defies answer by a timeless and abstract reason alone. Only historical eschatology can adequately tell us whether Christ fulfils Kṛṣṇa, or Kṛṣṇa, Christ or none supercedes the other. The

question *as such* is childish, as though I were to argue that my
daddy writes better poetry than your daddy (forgetting that
each poem is unique for each child and there can be no
comparing of poems qua poems). *In you* and *in me* the question
is premature (neither of us need be argued out of his belief); *in
us*—i.e., insofar as it helps us toward mutual understanding
and the ultimate goal of all mankind—history (personal and
collective) will have the last word. Meanwhile a wholesome
emulation will harm neither side. Things might go farther; the
Vaisnava may perhaps admit the also historical nature of
Krsna, thereby opening the door for the Christian to acknowledge the growth—hence the metamorphosis—Christ
'undergoes' down the ages. The Christian may perhaps admit
the also transhistorical nature of Christ, thereby opening the
door for the Vaisnava to acknowledge the mystery—hence
the pluriformity—Krsna 'undergoes' down the ages. But this
is only a beginning, because the continuation of the dialogue
has to produce its own rules and categories.

10.　FAITH AND BELIEFS

I need hardly say that neither every Vaisnava nor every
Christian is automatically prepared, in intellect and spirit, to
come thus face to face—at bottom because very few have had
the experience and so it has not been worked out theologically. Here history might teach a mighty lesson by reminding
us how Jewish, Greek, Zoroastrian and other 'dogmas' seeped
into the Christian mind, making themselves part of what we
nowadays call the common Christian heritage. The same
would apply for a theology of Krsna—in both cases.

For the moment let us content ourselves with some philosophical and theological considerations centering on the distinction we have drawn between faith and belief. For the sake
of simplicity I shall start from Christian assumptions that
commend themselves as a succinct and intelligible frame of
reference to the Western mind, but that can be readily trans-
posed into those of other religious traditions. Let me add at
once that in so doing I jump to no conclusions as to whether

the Christian approach can be universalized in a way others cannot. At the present time I do not wish to grapple with that problem.

The main function of faith is to connect me with transcendence, with what stands above me, with what I am not (yet). Faith is the connection with the beyond, however you choose to envision it. So one thing faith effects is salvation: The business of faith is preeminently to save Man. Now for this, faith cannot be couched in universal forms that express it fully. If this were possible, faith would become so earthbound that it would no longer provide a bridge 'binding' us (Latin *religare*) to something loftier than ourselves. Faith may lend itself more or less to ideation, but no set of words, no expression, can ever exhaust it. And yet it needs to be embodied in ideas and formulas—so much so that faith incapable of expressing itself at all would not be human faith. Such expressions we have called beliefs, in accordance with what tradition has always felt.

Were things otherwise, my faith would cut me off from Men rather than unite me with them, faith would estrange Men instead of binding them together and religion would express horizontal divergences instead of vertical convergence. That history, for countless reasons, bears witness to both trends in the actual evolution of religions does not invalidate what I am saying; it only shows that faith has been confused with belief. The moment dialogue ceases and Men live isolated from one another, faith inevitably becomes identified with belief and fosters exclusivism with all the results that history in general and the history of religions in particular have made so painfully familiar.

Yet our distinction presents special features. Faith cannot be equated with belief, but faith always needs a belief to be faith. Belief is not faith, but it must convey faith. A disembodied faith is not faith. A belief that does not always point to a beyond that outsoars and in a sense annihilates it is not belief but fanaticism. Faith finds expression in belief, and through it Men normally arrive at faith. Where Men live in a homogeneous cultural world, most never notice the tension between faith and belief. They look on dogmas, which are simply authoritative formulations of belief, almost as if they were faith itself, half-forgetting that they are dogmas *of* faith. When cultural change or an encounter between religions robs the notions hitherto bound up with faith of their solidity and unmistakable correspondence to faith, naturally a crisis erupts. But this is a crisis of belief, not faith. Undoubtedly the bond between the two is intimate; it is in fact constitutive, since thought itself requires language, and belief is the language of faith. Hence what begins as a crisis of belief turns into a crisis of faith, as a rule due to the intransigence of those who will tolerate no change because they do not distinguish between faith and belief.

When a Christian says he believes in God the Father, in Christ and in the Holy Spirit, he does not believe in a *deus ex machina ad usum christianorum*, but a reality of truth subsisting everywhere, even outside the bounds of his own experience. But he conveys this truth in language inherited from his own tradition, and he can grasp its meaning only in those terms. When he comes into contact with a different form of religious expression, his first impulse will be to suppose his interlocutor is talking about some reality apart from and essentially different from his own: He will think of false 'gods', false religion and so on. After a deeper look, he will perceive that at bottom they mean a similar thing, although the other refers to it with concepts he may judge inadequate or erroneous. Thus one of the primary tasks facing theology is the tremendous one of finding parallels and features in other religions that complement each other, as well as points of conflict. But no one can deny the ultimate purpose of the two religions is the same. Unless the spadework, entailing all we have indicated, is done at the outset, and a good deal more besides, misunderstandings will almost inevitably accumulate, even today, to bedevil nine tenths of the relations among religions and therefore among Men.

At times the obvious will have to be explained, but patience seems to be an intellectual as well as a moral virtue. Doesn't faith itself call on Man to break out of his limitations

and constantly die to himself to rise again in newness of life? I
mean that the Christian's connatural attitude toward the faith
of others seems to embrace, absorb and embody rather than
repulse, expel and shut out. Possibly these are two anthropological bents marking different cultural situations; but
in any event the disposition to attract rather than repel strikes
me as more consonant with the Christian dynamism.

I shall not attempt now to develop an entire doctrine of
the Mystery—whom Christians recognize in Christ and other
religions in other symbols—present and at work in every
religion, usually in a dark and enigmatic way. I will only try to
set forth the spiritual attitude that impels me to seek to integrate, as far as possible, other Men's religiousness into my own
before asserting mine in order to compare and judge. Let a
Man only dip into the experience of trying to understand a
form of religion from inside, and he will perceive the authen-
ticity and truth with which it is charged, whatever the weakness and even immorality its outward features exhibit (as in a
certain worship or Kṛṣṇa or certain interpretations of Christianity). What I should like to stress is the way faith prompts
one to link up different kinds of religion. Men may not see
eye-to-eye about how to do this, but theology today must
work out the means if it is to survive and stop being archaeol-
ogy.

The solution is not so easy, not only due to historical and
cultural estrangements, but also because the relation between
faith and belief is not so simple that we might consider belief
the mere costume of faith and so infer that it is all a matter of
taste for one vestment or another. Belief, the garb or expression of faith, is part and parcel of faith itself inasmuch as Man's
self-understanding belongs to the very nature of that being
whose nature is precisely understanding—even if it is not
exclusively understanding. I cannot strip off my belief—
insofar as it is a real belief, i.e., insofar as I believe in 'it' (or
more simply said, I believe)—without touching and even
transforming my faith.

In a word, I am not simplistically saying that all beliefs are merely expressions of one and the same faith, because faith without belief does not exist—not for those who believe. Man is not *logos* alone, but the *logos* is something more than the mere instrument of Man. This is why to speak of the transcendent unity of religions is true as long as it does not remain the immanent 'truth' of the different religious traditions under discussion.[8] The *relativity* of beliefs does not mean their *relativism*. Our human task is to establish a religious dialogue that, although it transcends the *logos*—and belief—does not neglect or ignore them.

I am only trying to say that faith must not be confused with belief. Many a misunderstanding has risen from confusing them, or rather from not adequately distinguishing between them.

The experience of faith is a primal anthropological act that every person performs in one way or another, rather like the way we begin to use reason upon its awakening, although no one can foresee along what lines our minds will work or what our first thoughts will be. The act of faith itself has saving power. Theologians will hasten to say (and we need not contradict them) that the act of faith can be made by a human being only when God's grace prompts him to make it. In any event the act of faith is not only transcendent, uniting us with what surpasses us, but also transcendental. It exceeds all possible formulations, and it makes them possible because it also precedes them. Faith is a constitutive human dimension.[9]

At any rate the experience of faith is a human experience that will not be contained in any formula but in fact couches itself in what I have called formulas of belief. Man perforce gives utterance to the deepest of his impressions, but to this end he must use language that binds it up with a given human tradition, he lays hold of images and symbols that belong to his cultural group. He will make his faith known in a set of beliefs that he will perhaps call dogmas, expressing in intellectual terms what he wishes to convey. Obviously these terms may be multifarious; in fact they are necessarily pluralistic.

I am not suggesting that all beliefs are equal and interchangeable; I am saying that in a certain respect they exhibit the same nature, which makes dialogue, and even dialectics, possible. Moreover, I assert they are generally equivalent in that every belief has a similar function: to express Man's faith, that faith which is the anthropological dimension through which Man reaches his goal—in Christian language, his salvation.

Clearly there remains the major difficulty of ascertaining how deep each belief delves into faith or how satisfactorily it expresses faith. Certain creedal formulas deriving from a naive, underdeveloped cast of mind may not answer the needs of more highly developed people. This truth emerges at every turn in the history of religions, in the encounter and cross-fertilization between differing religious traditions, in the dialogue and sometimes the skirmishes between different schools of thought within the same tradition. We have an example of it in much of what goes on in the cultural and religious world of the Catholicism people call 'Roman': The noble monolithic solidity of that world breaks down into various parts, into all the colors of the rainbow, through a thoroughgoing change of beliefs within a single experience of faith.

The problem we are considering reaches far beyond these limits and lights on the farthest human horizon where the issue of religious encounter presents itself. For obvious reasons we can only rough out the problem here. One way or another we are all embarked on the venture. Dead calm is as fraught with danger as a roaring gale. While we are on the high seas we must have oars and sails.

NOTES

1. No need to remind the reader that *parish*, Latin *paroecia*, comes from the Greek πάροικος, from παρά and οίκος, to sojourn, dwell beside, be

beside the house, a neighbor, but also a stranger. Cf. πάροχος, a public purveyor.

2. Cf. R. Panikkar, *Myth, Faith and Hermeneutics* (New York: Paulist Press 1978), chapter XIV on *karma,* which expands this example.

3. Cf. ibid. chapter VI.

4. Cf. R. Panikkar, 'Verstehen als Ueberzeugstein' in *Neue Anthropologie*, vol. 7, edited by H.G. Gadamer and P. Vogler (Stuttgart: Thieme, 1975), pp. 132-67.

5. Cf. *Myth, Faith and Hermeneutics, op. cit.,* chapter IX.

6. Cf. chapter III.

7. Cf. the two following quotations, the first of Thomas Aquinas citing St. Ambrose (Glossa Lombardi, P.L. 191, 1651): "Omne verum, a quocumque dicatur, a Spiritu Sancto est." *Summa Theologiae* I-II. q. 109, a. 1, ad 1. And the second from Meister Eckhart: "False vero, a quocumque dicatur, nulli dicitur." In Iohan. I, 51 (Nr. 277 of the Opera omnia). Cf. also *Sermo* XX (Nr. 198).

8. Cf. F. Schuon, *De l'unité transcendante des religions* (Paris: Gallimard, 1948) of which there is an English translation (London: Faber and Faber, 1953) and which has recently been resurrected in the North American scene (cf. *Journal of the American Academy of Religion,* XLIV, 4; December 1976, pp. 715-724).

9. Cf. *Myth, Faith and Hermeneutics, op. cit.,* chapter VI.

II. THE RULES OF THE GAME IN THE RELIGIOUS ENCOUNTER

śāstra-yonitvāt
Learned traditions being the
source (of knowledge).
                    BS I, 1, 3 (+)

+ 'Brahman is the *yoni* of the *śāstras*' says Śaṅkara in his commentary. The
Great Scriptures, the human traditions are the womb of knowledge and
brahman also the source not in a vicious, but in a vital circle.

The meeting of religions is an inescapable fact today. I would like to formulate one principle that should govern the meeting of religions, and draw from it a few corollary consequences.

The principle is this: *The Religious encounter must be a truly religious one.* Anything short of this simply will not do.

Some consequences are the following:

1. IT MUST BE FREE FROM PARTICULAR APOLOGETICS

If the Christian or Buddhist or believer in whatever religion approaches another religious person with the a priori idea of defending his own religion by all (obviously honest) means, we shall have perhaps a valuable defense of that religion and undoubtedly exciting discussions, but no religious dialogue, no encounter, much less a mutual enrichment and fecundation. One need not give up one's beliefs and convictions — surely not, but we must eliminate any apologetics if we really want to meet a person from another religious tradition. By apologetics I understand that part of the science of a particular religion that tends to prove the truth and value of that religion. Apologetics has its function and its proper place, but not here in the meeting of religions.

2. IT MUST BE FREE FROM GENERAL APOLOGETICS

I understand very well the anguish of the modern religious person seeing the wave of 'unreligion' and even 'irreligion' in our times, and yet I would consider it misguided to fall prey to such a fear by founding a kind of religious league—not to say crusade—of the 'pious', of religious people of all confessions, defenders of the 'sacred rights' of religion.

If to forget the first corollary would indicate a lack of confidence in our partner and imply that he is wrong and that I must 'convert' him, to neglect this second point would betray a lack of confidence in the truth of religion itself and represent an indiscriminate accusation against 'modern' Man. The attitude proposing a common front for religion or against unbelief may be understandable, but it is not a religious attitude—not according to the present degree of religious consciousness.

3. ONE MUST FACE THE CHALLENGE OF CONVERSION

If the encounter is to be an authentically religious one, it must be totally loyal to truth and open to reality. The genuinely religious spirit is not loyal only to the past, it also keeps faith with the present. A religious Man is neither a fanatic nor someone who already has all the answers. He also is a seeker, a pilgrim making his own uncharted way; the track ahead is yet virgin, inviolate. The religious Man finds each moment new and is but the more pleased to see in this both the beauty of a personal discovery and the depth of a perennial treasure that his ancestors in the faith have handed down.

And yet, to enter the new field of the religious encounter is a challenge and a risk. The religious person enters this arena without prejudices and preconceived solutions, knowing full well he may in fact have to lose a particular belief or particular religion altogether. He trusts in truth. He enters unarmed and ready to be converted himself. He may lose his life—he may also be born again.

4. THE HISTORICAL DIMENSION IS NECESSARY BUT NOT SUFFICIENT

Religion is not just *Privatsache*, nor just a vertical 'link' with the Absolute, but it is also a connection with mankind; it has a tradition, a historical dimension. The religious encounter is not merely the meeting of two or more people in their capacity as strictly private individuals, severed from their respective religious traditions. A truly religious Man bears at once the burden of tradition and the riches of his ancestors. But he is not an official representative, as it were, speaking only on behalf of others or from sheer hearsay: He is a living member of a community, a believer in a living religious tradition.

The religious encounter must deal with the historical dimension, not stop with it. It is not an encounter of historians, still less of archeologists; but a living dialogue, a place for creative thinking and imaginative new ways that do not break with the past but continue and extend it.

This is hardly to disparage historical considerations; quite the contrary, I would insist on an understanding of the traditions in question that is at once deep and broad. The first implies not only that we be familiar with the age-old tradition, but also with the present state of that particular religion. Taking as our example that bundle of religions which goes under the name of 'Hinduism', I would contend that a profound understanding of this tradition cannot ignore its evolution up to the present day, unless we are ready to accept an arbitrary and skewed interpretation. A scholar may indeed limit himself to Vedic studies, for example, but someone engaged in a truly religious encounter can scarcely justify basing his understanding of Hinduism solely on Sāyana's interpretation of the Vedas while completely ignoring that of, say, Dayānānda or Aurobindo (the relative merits of various interpretations is not our concern here). Similarly no modern Christian can be satisfied with Jerome's interpretation of the Bible, or with the mediaeval understanding of it.

Our point is that no study of an idea, cultural pattern or religious tradition is adequate unless we consider all its possibilities, just as no botanist can claim to know a seed until he knows the plant that grows up from that seed. Moreover, in this case, the movement of understanding is dynamic and reciprocal. Thus I would contend not only that any study of the nature of *dharma*, for instance, is incomplete if it does not consider the present-day understanding of that concept, but also that the ancient notion is likely to be only partially understood if its development up to modern times is left aside. This also implies that someone who tries to understand the notion of *dharma*, whether in ancient or modern India, cannot do so *in vacuo*: the very words he uses are already culturally charged with meanings and values.

Further, the traditions must also be understood in a broader perspective, one that oversteps the provincial boundaries of geography and culture. To understand the Hindu tradition—staying with our example—we cannot limit ourselves to the Indian subcontinent: The impact of Buddhism on eastern and central Asia is so well known that I need only mention it; the Rāmāyāna and the Mahābhārata have been shaping forces in many countries south of Burma; Śiva is worshiped in Indonesia. Pursuing these avenues of research is not a mere academic tangent, but serves to complete the picture we begin to see through indigenous sources. Even more, we cannot limit our attention to past cross-cultural contacts, and ignore the multitude of contemporary instances. Many an Indian value asserts itself today on the shores of California and in universities throughout Europe. Whether the change in climate distorts or enhances the original values is a separate question; the influence is unmistakable. In return, Western values have, for better or for worse, deeply penetrated not only the great cities but also the most remote villages of India. Given such developments, can our understanding of Indian religions remain imprisoned in a scholarly ivory tower whose drawbridge was raised when the Muslims arrived? The phenomenon of feedback does not refer only to the diffusion of gadgets and other technological paraphernalia throughout the world; popularized ideas from every continent now travel literally at the speed of light to the farthest corners of the planet and the deepest recesses of the human psyche.

The importance of the historical dimension notwithstanding, what is at stake in the religious encounter is not 'History of Religions' or even 'Comparative Religion', but a living and demanding faith. Faith is life and life cannot be reduced to imitating the past or merely reinterpreting it. The religious encounter is a religious event.

5. IT IS NOT JUST A CONGRESS OF PHILOSOPHY

Needless to say, without a certain degree of philosophy no encounter is possible, and yet the religious dialogue is not just a meeting of philosophers to discuss intellectual problems. Religions are much more than doctrines. Within one religion there may even be a pluralism of doctrines. To pin down a religion to a certain definite doctrinal set is to kill that religion. No particular doctrine *as such* can be considered the unique and irreplaceable expression of a religion. Indeed, *denying* a particular doctrine without overcoming it or substituting another for it may be heresy, but no religion is satisfied to be *only* orthodoxy, ignoring orthopraxis. To be sure, creation, God, *nirvāṇa* and the like are important concepts, but the real religious issue lies elsewhere: in the real 'thing' meant by these and other notions. I may share with my Muslim colleague the same idea of the transcendence of God and he may be of the same opinion as his Buddhist partner regarding the law of *karma* and yet none of us may feel compelled to change his religion.

Clearly, I need to understand what the other is saying, that is, what he means to say, and this involves a new understanding of interpretation itself. Now the golden rule of any hermeneutic is that the interpreted thing can recognize itself in the interpretation. In other words, any interpretation from outside a tradition has to coincide, at least phenomenologically, with an interpretation from within, i.e., with the believer's viewpoint. To label a *mūrtipūjaka* an idol-worshiper, for instance, using idol as it is commonly understood in the Judeo-Christian-Muslim context rather than beginning with what the worshiper affirms of himself, is to transgress this rule.

An entire philosophical and religious context underpins the notion of *mūrti*; we cannot simply impose alien categories on it. Although the problem remains formidable, one of the most positive achievements of our times is that we have come to realize that there are no immutable categories that can serve as absolute criteria for judging everything under the sun.

Briefly then, I would like to consider two principles that govern any sound hermeneutical method and the way in which they may be critically coordinated.

The *principle of homogeneity*: An ancient conviction, held in both East and West, has it that only like can know like. In other words, a concept can be properly understood and evaluated only from within a homogeneous context. Every cultural value has a definite sphere where it is valid and meaningful; any unwarranted extrapolation can only lead to confusion and misunderstanding. Nothing is more harmful than hurried syntheses or superficial parallelisms. Here is the place and the great value of traditional theology, which provides the internal understanding of a religion, the self-understanding of that religion as it is lived. Without this previous work, fruitful interreligious encounters would not be possible.

The *dialogical principle*: Applying the principle of homogeneity with strict rigor or exclusivity would paralyze a critical approach and halt any progress toward mutual understanding. I may understand the world view that underlies the religious practice of another—human sacrifice, for instance—yet I may still consider it immature, wrong, even barbaric. Why is this? It may be that I have developed another form of awareness or discovered another principle of understanding that leads me to see the inadequacy of a certain notion (here that which upholds human sacrifice). I may have acquired a perspective under which I am able to criticize another point of view; perhaps I can now detect incongruencies or assumptions that are no longer tenable. In this sort of activity, the dialogical principle is at work. Only through an internal or external dialogue can we become aware of uncritical or unwarranted assumptions. This dialogue does not merely look for new sources of information, but leads to a deeper understanding of the other and of oneself. We are all learning to welcome light and criticism, even when it comes from foreign shores.

Co-ordination: By themselves, each of these principles is barren and unsatisfying; together they provide a means of cross-cultural understanding that is both valid and critical. Those concerned with Indian traditions, whatever their background, are convinced that they cannot disregard the methodological principles of modern critical scholarship. At the same time, they are quite aware that neither science nor Western categories constitute an absolute standard, nor do they have universal applicability. These two insights give rise to the coordination of the two principles. Here we cannot elaborate the guidelines for such a coordination. It is enough to say that the effort must be truly interdisciplinary and interpersonal, involving not only the traditional fields of 'academia', but also the people whose religions we are considering. No statement is valid and meaningful if it cannot be heard, understood and, in a way, verified by all those concerned, and not merely bandied about by the *literati*.

Indeed, philosophical clarification is today extremely important since by and large religions have lived in restricted areas and closed circles, and have tended to identify a particular set of philosophical doctrines—because they were useful to convey the religious message—with the core of the religion. The mutual enrichment of real encounter and the consequent liberation may be enormous.

6. IT IS NOT ONLY A THEOLOGICAL SYMPOSIUM

As an authentic venture, the true religious encounter is filled with a sort of prophetic charisma; it is not just an effort to make the outsider understand my point. Indeed, at least according to more than one school, true theology also claims to be a charismatic deepening in meaning of a particular revelation or religion. Generally, however, theologians are more concerned with explaining given data than with exploring tasks ahead. Obviously hermeneutics is indispensable; but still more important is to *grasp* what is to be interpreted prior to any (more or less plausible) explanation. Theology may furnish the tools for mutual understanding but must remember that the religious encounter imperative today is a new problem, and that the tools furnished by the theologies are not fit to master the new task unless purified, chiseled and perhaps forged anew in the very encounter.

As an example of what is needed, we may use the notion of homology, which does not connote a mere comparison of concepts from one tradition with those of another. I want to suggest this notion as the correlation between points of two different systems so that a point in one system corresponds to a point in the other. The method does not imply that one system is better (logically, morally or whatever) than the other, nor that the two points are interchangeable: You cannot, as it were, transplant a point from one system to the other. The method only discovers homologous correlations.

Now a homology is not identical to an analogy, although they are related. Homology does not mean that two notions are analogous, i.e., partially the same and partially different, since this implies that both share in a 'tertiam quid' that provides the basis for the analogy. Homology means rather that the notions play equivalent roles, that they occupy homologous places within their respective systems. Homology is perhaps a kind of existential-functional analogy.

An example may clarify what I mean.

It is quite clearly false, for instance, to equate the upaniṣadic concept of *Brahman* with the biblical notion of *Yahweh*. Nevertheless it is equally unsatisfactory to say that these concepts have nothing whatever in common. True, their context and contents are utterly different, they are not mutually translatable, nor do they have a direct relationship. But they are homologous, each plays a similar role, albeit in different cultural settings. They both refer to a highest value and an absolute term. On the other hand, we cannot say that *Brahman* is provident and even transcendent, or that *Yahweh* is all-pervading, without attributes, etc. Nevertheless we can assert that both function homologously within their own cultures.

Or, to give another example, an examination of the traditional Indian notion of *karma* and the modern Western understanding of historicity under the aegis of this principle could reveal a common homologous role: Each one stands for that temporal ingredient of the human being which transcends individuality.[1] Even more intriguing, perhaps, would be a consideration that homologizes the Indian notion of Īśvara (Lord) and the Western idea of Christ.[2]

Whatever shape it will take, whatever contents it will carry, I am convinced that a new theology (though this very name means nothing to a Buddhist) will emerge precisely out of these encounters between sincere and enlightened believers of the various religious traditions.

Yet the religious encounter is not a mere theological reflection. Theologies—in the widest sense of the word—have a given basis: They are efforts at intelligibility of a given religious tradition and generally within that tradition itself (*fides quaerens intellectum*). But here we do not have such a belief or such a basis. There is neither a common given nor an accepted basis, revelation, event or even tradition. Both the very subject matter and the method are to be determined in the encounter itself. There is no common language at the outset. Short of this radical understanding the encounter of religions becomes a mere cultural entertainment.

7. IT IS NOT MERELY AN ECCLESIASTICAL ENDEAVOR

To be sure, the dialogue among religions may take place at different levels and on each level it has its peculiarities. Official encounter among representatives of the world's organized religious groups is today an inescapable duty. Yet the issues in such meetings are not the same as those in a dialogue that tries to reach the deepest possible level. Ecclesiastical dignitaries are bound to preserve tradition; they must consider the multitude of believers who follow that religion, for and to whom they are responsible. They are faced with practical and immediate problems, they must discover ways to tolerate, to collaborate, to understand. But in general they cannot risk new solutions. They have to approve and put into practice already proven fruitful ways. But where are those proofs to come from? The religious encounter we have in mind will certainly pave the way for ecclesiastical meetings and vice versa, but must be differentiated and separated from them.

8. IT IS A RELIGIOUS ENCOUNTER IN FAITH, HOPE AND LOVE

I apologize for the Christian overtones of this terminology and yet I think its meaning is universal.

By *faith* I mean an attitude that transcends the simple data, and the dogmatic formulations of the different confessions as well; that attitude which reaches an understanding even when words and concepts differ, because it pierces them, as it were, goes deep down to that realm which is the religious realm par excellence. We do not discuss systems but realities, and the way in which these realities manifest themselves so that they also make sense for our partner.

By *hope* I understand that attitude which, hoping against all hope, is able to leap over not only the initial human obstacles, our weakness and unconscious adherences, but also over all kinds of purely profane views and into the heart of the dialogue, as if urged from above to perform a sacred duty.

By *love*, finally, I mean that impulse, that force impelling us to our fellow-beings and leading us to discover in them what is lacking in us. To be sure, real love does not aim for victory in the encounter. It longs for common recognition of the truth, without blotting out the differences or muting the various melodies in the single polyphonic symphony.

9. APPENDIX
a. Some Practical Lessons

What do these rules mean in practice? The chief lessons gleaned from my experience could be summarized as follows:

There must be *equal preparation* for the encounter on both sides, and this means cultural as well as theological preparation. Any dialogue—including the religious one—depends on the cultural settings of the partners. To overlook the cultural differences that give rise to different religious beliefs is to court unavoidable misunderstandings. The first function of the dialogue is to discover the ground where the dialogue may properly take place.

There must be real *mutual trust* between those involved in the encounter, something that is possible only when all the cards are on the table, i.e., when neither partner 'brackets' his personal beliefs.[3]

The *different issues* (theological, practical, institutional, etc.) have to be carefully distinguished; otherwise there is going to be confusion.

b. A Christian Example

Christ is the Lord, but the Lord is neither only Jesus nor does my understanding exhaust the meaning of the word.

Church, as the sociological dimension of religion, is the organism of salvation (by definition); but the Church is not coextensive with the visible Christian Church.

Christendom is the socio-religious structure of Christianity and as such is a religion like any other. It must be judged on its own merits without any special privileges.

God wills that all Men should reach salvation. Here salvation is that which is considered to be the end, goal, destination or destiny of Man, however this may be conceived.

There is no salvation without faith, but this is not the privilege of Christians, nor of any special group.

The means of salvation are to be found in any authentic religion (old or new), since a Man follows a particular religion because in it he believes he finds the ultimate fulfillment of his life.

Christ is the only mediator, but he is not the monopoly of Christians and, in fact, he is present and effective in any authentic religion, whatever the form or the name. Christ is the symbol, which Christians call by this name, of the ever-transcending but equally ever-humanly immanent Mystery. Now these principles should be confronted with parallel Humanist, Buddhist and other principles, and then one should be able to detect points of convergence and of discrepancy with all the required qualifications. Further, the Christian principles have no a priori paradigmatic value, so that it is not a question of just searching for possible equivalents elsewhere. The fair procedure is to start from all possible starting points and witness to the actual encounters taking place along the way.

c. Summing up

The religious encounter is a religious, and hence sacred, act through which we are taken up by the truth and by loyalty to the 'three worlds' with no further aim or intention. In this creative religious act the very vitality of religion manifests itself.

NOTES

1. Cf. R. Panikkar, *Myth, Faith and Hermeneutics* (New York: Paulist Press, 1978), chapter XIV.
2. Cf. R. Panikkar, *The Unknown Christ of Hinduism* (London: Darton, Longman & Todd, 1964), pp. 119-131.
3. Cf. The next chapter.

III. EPOCHÉ
in the Religious Encounter

Nothing is more outwardly visible than
the secrets of the heart,
nothing more obvious than what one
attempts to conceal.

Chung Yung I, 1, 3 (+)

+ Ezra Pound's translation.

1. PROLOGUE

Interreligious dialogue is today unavoidable; it is a religious imperative and a historical duty for which we must suitably prepare. But we often hear more talk about interreligious dialogue than actual dialogue. In order to sidestep this pitfall, I would like to begin by stressing the often-neglected notion of an *intrareligious* dialogue, i.e., an inner dialogue within myself, an encounter in the depth of my personal religiousness, having met another religious experience on that very intimate level. In other words, if *interreligious* dialogue is to be real dialogue, an *intrareligious* dialogue must accompany it, i.e., it must begin with my questioning myself and the *relativity* of my beliefs (which does not mean their *relativism*), accepting the challenge of a change, a conversion and the risk of upsetting my traditional patterns. *Quaestio mihi factus sum*, 'I have made a question of myself', said that great African Augustine. One simply cannot enter the arena of genuine religious dialogue without such a self-critical attitude.

My point is this: I shall never be able to meet the other as he meets and understands himself if I do not meet and understand him in and as myself. To understand the other as 'other' is, at the least, not to understand him as he understands him-self (which is certainly not as 'other', but as self). Obviously this self that understands the other is not my previous *ego* that reduces the other to my own unchanged self. Each process of real understanding changes me as much as it changes the other. Real understanding transforms my *ego* as well as the *alius*. The meeting point—and this is my thesis—is not a

40

neutral dialectical arena that leaves both of us untouched, but a self that besides being myself is also shared by the other. This is to say, among other things, that I am not advocating any reductionism. I have developed this point elsewhere; here I am only concerned to pave the way for such an approach by dismissing as insufficient a minimalistic attitude without, obviously, falling into the trap of exclusivism.

In a laudable effort to avoid an exclusivist and paternalist posture, some modern writers are tempted by the *phenomenological epoché,* improperly so-called in this context, which is interpreted to be the bracketing of one's 'faith' as the necessary condition for fruitful 'interfaith dialogue'.

This attitude is more common than we usually suppose, although not always under the aegis of so scientific an expression. When a Christian, for example, thinks he can understand another religion or be a partner in dialogue without engaging his own religious convictions, he is trying to practice this kind of *epoché.* When a Hindu thinks he can genuinely experience another religion just by experimenting, by accepting—for the time being and the sake of the experiment—the rites, practices and beliefs of the other, he too is intending to bracket his 'faith' by the *epoché* we are discussing. Has the Hindu really bracketed his convictions when he claims to follow the Christian path for a time? Has the Christian shut off his Christian faith when he tries to forget his beliefs or preferences and accommodate himself to the forms and habits of another tradition? No one today, I guess, would say that Ramakrishna Paramahamsa or Roberto de Nobili practiced *epoché* when they sincerely tried to enter the heart of another religion. Rather, they were impelled by a belief that their personal religion was wide enough and deep enough to allow such an embrace.

2. CRITIQUE OF THE SO-CALLED PHENOMENOLOGICAL 'EPOCHÉ' IN THE RELIGIOUS ENCOUNTER

I shall offer here only some critical considerations of this attitude without, I hasten to add, tackling just now the many other problems involved in the phenomenology and philosophy of religious dialogue.

Although this chapter seems to have a negative character because it attempts to dispel a misunderstanding, it actually offers a positive standpoint, namely that inner dialogue involving the whole person is the necessary condition for a real and fruitful encounter of religions.

The opinion I am going to criticize understands *epoché* as putting aside one's personal religious convictions, suspending judgment on the validity of one's own religious tenets; in a word, bracketing the concrete beliefs of individual allegiance to a particular confession.

The good intention underlying this attitude is obvious: the *epoché* is put forward in order to prevent undue dominance from any one side, or to be able to understand better, without bias or prejudice. The *epoché* would thus provide a common ground, a necessary condition for genuine dialogue in which neither side predominates. It is feared that if I approach my partner with strong personal convictions, either I shall not be able to listen to, much less understand, him, her or it, filled as I am with my own tenets, or we shall be unable to find a common language.

If I believe in God or Christ or *karma*, for instance, and my partner does not, unless for the sake of dialogue I 'put off my belief in God, Christ or *karma*, we shall not be able to establish a real dialogue without privileges on either side. So it is said. The *epoché* procedure has been compared to a kind of methodological doubt. I temporarily suspend my judgment about some fundamental tenets I hold true, bracket my personal 'faith', because I do not want to impose it on my partner nor influence him in the least regarding the contents of our dialogue. Thus I am ready to meet him on his own ground, having renounced my personal standing.

The positive aspect of such an attempt lies in the fact that it distinguishes between the conceptualized beliefs of a person and the underlying existential faith. If the subject matter of the *epoché* consists of the concepts we form about a particular idea, then we should be able to perform and even welcome such an operation. The problem arises when we pretend to bracket not a formulation, a notion, but a fundamental conviction of the person at the existential level. If we accept the distinction between faith and belief, we may be able to agree to a certain necessary *epoché* of our beliefs, but I would prefer to call for transcending them altogether as long as we are engaged in a serious interreligious dialogue. The *epoché* looks rather like a closet for temporarily storing one's personal convictions for the sake of the dialogue; whereas transcending our concepts is not simply a methodological device. A nonconceptual awareness allows different translations of the same transconceptual reality for different notional systems without methodological strategies.

The need and the place for a truly phenomenological *epoché* comes in the introductory stage, getting to know a particular religiousness by means of an unbiased description of its manifestations.

a. Negative

My contention is that transferring the *epoché* to a field not its own, like that of ultimate convictions in the interreligious dialogue, would be:

> psychologically impracticable,
> phenomenologically inappropriate,
> philosophically defective,
> theologically weak
> and religiously barren.

Before taking up the burden of proof, I wish to state emphatically, although very concisely, that I am not:

> speaking against phenomenology in general or against phenomenology of religion, which has its own merits and justification since there is room for a clear and valid description of religious phenomena;

> attacking authentic phenomenological *epoché* or finding this procedure incorrect in phenomenological analysis;

> belittling all the steps prior and necessary to an inter-

religious dialogue; human sympathy, for instance, capacity and willingness to listen and learn, sincere desire to understand, conscious effort to overcome preconceptions, etc.;

advocating sticking to one's own judgment about the other's religiousness or not performing a phenomenological reduction of my preconceptions regarding the other. I am not saying, for example, that a Protestant should from the outset judge a Roman Catholic idolatrous because of the Marian cult.

b. Positive
On the contrary, I am saying that:

precisely what I should not and cannot put into brackets are my religious convictions, my ultimate religious evaluations, for I must approach religious dialogue without putting my most intimate self on some safe ground outside the confrontation and challenge of the dialogue;

dialogue is neither teaching nor simply listening; in other words, interreligious dialogue presupposes a rather advanced stage in the confrontation between people of different religious allegiances. Obviously, before meaningful dialogue can take place one must already know the religion of the partner. But one must be both intellectually and spiritually prepared. Dialogue is not mere study or understanding (although, indeed, by dialogue I may well deepen my understanding of my partner), but a total human contrast and participation in deeper communication and fuller communion;

interreligious dialogue demands a mutual confrontation of everything we are, believe and believe we are, in order to establish that deeper human fellowship without prejudicing the results, without precluding any possible transformation of our personal religiousness.

3. THESIS: THE PHENOMENOLOGICAL 'EPOCHÉ' IS OUT OF PLACE IN THE RELIGIOUS ENCOUNTER
a. Such an *epoché* is *psychologically impracticable* if religious dialogue is to be more than merely doctrinal discussion, i.e., if

it is a personal encounter with the whole human being. It would be pretense to affirm that I do not know or am not convinced of my certainties. I cannot simply abstract my deepest convictions or concoct the fiction that I have forgotten or laid aside what I hold to be true. Just this would be required if I really had to bracket my 'faith'.

If for instance I am convinced that God created the world or that the law of *karma* is true, I cannot act (and dialogue is action) *as if* I did not believe in these tenets. Even if I sincerely tried to bracket these convictions, they would go on conditioning and generating a score of side issues. My partner simply would not understand why I maintain the fundamental goodness of this world against empirical evidence, or why I see congruences where he does not, etc. In other words, every reason I might adduce in our discussion regarding the ultimate nature of the world or human behavior would spring from my repressed convictions (existence of a creator, validity of the karmic line, etc.).

Imagine I am reading a detective story. Just when I am at the climax, someone who has read the novel tells me 'who done it'. I cannot continue reading *as if* I did not know. Not only are the charm, interest and tension gone; the reading becomes insipid, or at least qualitatively different. If I still read on, my interest will shift to checking plot consistency, the writer's skill, style, and so on.

On the contrary, the genuine phenomenological *epoché* is psychologically possible because it does not engage the entire *psyche*, the whole person; it is an intellectual attitude adopted to get at the phenomenon with the requisite accuracy. I can remain immobile if I like while speaking, but I must open and close my arms to embrace somebody.

b. This method is also *phenomenologically inappropriate*, and this for several reasons:

to ask for the psychological inhibition required to lock up all my religious convictions for the time being—when it is no longer a question of description and understanding but of confrontation and dialogue—is almost an offense against phenomenology, as if the latter feared our psychological constitution. If there is a foe to the now classical phenomenology, it is the so-called psychologism. It could even be said—as the first volume of Husserl's *Logische Untersuchungen* shows—that phenomenology emerges out of the effort to overcome and discard the psychological constituent-aspects of human consciousness. Both, the subjective attitude and the objective projection, are overcome in phenomenology because they do not belong to the realm of 'transcendental consciousness', the only place where the 'appearance of the essences', i.e., of the phenomena, occurs. But dialogue comes only after the transcendental-phenomenological reduction has been used as a methodological device to discover the 'transcendental ego' or 'pure consciousness'.

Submitting religious dialogue to phenomenological analysis—something quite apart from existentially performing the religious dialogue itself—one discovers that if the rule of *epoché* were valid, it should also be applied to the partner's personal convictions, so that having thoroughly bracketed both sides, religious dialogue would be impossible. Such an analysis would still detect vestiges of a superiority complex on the part of whoever defends or practices this *epoché*: They think they can accommodate themselves to the mind of the other and put away their own preconceptions, while the partner is not asked to do so. I repeat: The phenomenological *epoché* has its place in the study and initial clarification of religious phenomena, but not in the actual performance of dialogue.

The authentic phenomenological *epoché*, further, does not bracket my convictions or my claim to truth. When dealing with the *noemata*, the essences given in the 'eidetic intuition', i.e., with the manifestation of pure objects in the 'transcendental consciousness', phenomenological investigation brackets the external 'existence' (outside the mind) of the idea described. This makes sense within the Husserlian framework, but extending the *epoché* outside the limits for which it is intended amounts to an unwarranted extrapolation.

Phenomenology, and this is not its least merit, teaches precision in philosophical and prephilosophical investigation. It aims to lay bare the phenomenon so as to have, first, an 'objective' description (as far as possible), and second, to allow well-founded and justified interpretation. Phenomenology teaches us to listen to the phenomenon and to approach it with a minimum of presuppositions.

Now it is phenomenologically wrong, which amounts to saying it is a methodological error, to leave outside the dialogue an essential part of its subject matter.

In a Hindu-Christian dialogue on the nature and role of grace, for instance, neither participant can meaningfully lock away—for security or whatever—his personal commitment to and belief in grace. Otherwise the 'dialogue' becomes one partner inspecting the other's opinions, and not a real existential exchange on the religious level.

As an analysis of the conditions for a meaningful *epoché* shows, the very possibility of the *epoché* rests on assumptions that do not exist in many cultures and religious traditions. There are, for example, systems of thought and ways of life that do not make room for such a distinction between my belief and the truth it embodies, much less for a separation between them. To understand what the *epoché* is about, and even more to perform it, a certain sort of mind is required, and also to some extent a particular culture, which cannot presume to universality. There are in fact many cultures and religions in which the distinction between the truth and one's conviction of it is not possible, nor between ideas and what they 'intend', the formulation and the formulated thing, etc.

c. This phenomenological *epoché* is *philosophically defective* when applied to religious dialogue.

First of all, Cartesian methodological doubt—whatever its other merits—is not applicable here. It would be a philosophical mistake. Nobody, not even a philosopher, can jump over his own shadow. You do not experiment with ultimate convictions. You experience them.

Ultimate convictions—and if they are religious they are

ultimate—cannot be bracketed; there is no *doer* left to perform such a maneuver. I have nothing with which to manipu-
late what is by definition ultimate. Were such manipulation
possible, it would mean either total suicide with no resurrection possible, or that my ultimate convictions are not ultimate,
for beyond them the manipulator would remain pulling the
strings.

If I believe in God, for example, I cannot pretend that I
do not believe in God or speak and act *as if* there were no God
when—by definition if I believe in him—it is God who lets
me speak and act. Even methodologically I cannot put him
aside when I am convinced that it is he who enables me to deny
or bracket him. The 'God' I can dismiss—even for a
moment—as an unnecessary hypothesis is undoubtedly not a
necessary Absolute.

We can obviously bracket formulations and stop pressing
certain points if we 'sense', whatever our motives, that they are
not opportune. But the *epoché* in question does not intend to
bracket only formulae. In other words, Descartes could very
methodically doubt everything but his own method.

Were such an *epoché* maintained, the dialogue would
not even reach the level of a philosophical encounter, for
philosophy implies and requires a sincere and unconditional
search for truth and there can be no such search if my truth is
removed from the sight of my partner, for fear of frightening
him with my convictions, or out of reverence for him, not
wanting to dazzle him with the abundant light I keep for
myself.

d. Such a procedure is *theologically weak*. Can I lay down
my 'faith'—even methodologically or 'strategically'—like a
hat?

This would imply:

There is no fundamental understanding possible, no
basic human accord unless I distance myself from any type of
faith, thus reducing faith to a kind of luxury. Faith would then
not be necessary for a full human life, since we claim to

encounter our fellow-being on the deepest religious level without it.

My particular faith is so one-sided, so limited, that it represents an obstacle to human understanding, something that must be locked away or banished to some distant chamber of my being if I am to seek universal fellowship with other humans. If I keep my faith in brackets it is doubtless because I think it does not foster religious understanding, probably because my partner is not enough advanced to bear the 'sublime heights' of my particular brand of 'faith', which I carefully try to withhold from his scrutiny.

It is not simply a question of human respect—in every sense—but of anthropological integrity. If faith is something a Man can discard with impunity so that he can still meet his fellow beings religiously, meaningfully and humanly, this amounts to affirming that what I happen to believe is simply superrogatory to my being and has no fundamental relevance for my humanity.

e. Finally, such an *epoché* would be *religiously barren*: at a stroke it would delete the very subject matter of the dialogue. If in the religious dialogue I meet a person belonging to another religious tradition, we do not meet just to talk about the weather or merely to discuss some noncommittal doctrinal points, but to speak of his and my own ultimate concerns, about our ultimate convictions, about how we see and understand life, death, God, Man, etc. If I come to the encounter devoid of any religious commitment, so open and fresh that I have nothing, nothing of my own to contribute—besides the unbearable pretension of such a claim—I shall have frustrated any possible religious dialogue. We should be discussing precisely what I have bracketed. In order not to 'hurt' the other fellow with my convictions (suspicious notion!), I offend him by pretending I can meet him without laying all my cards on the table. How am I going to talk about him? Shall I examine his religious feelings and opinions before the higher tribunal of my uncommitted, unattached and open attitude? Isn't the very opposite the case? Does this not betray an almost pathological attachment to my 'faith', such a fear of losing it that I dare not risk it, but prefer instead to preserve it under lock and key?

To exclude my religious convictions from religious dialogue is like renouncing the use of reason in order to enter a reasonable encounter.

4. TOWARDS A GENUINE RELIGIOUS ENCOUNTER

It is not the purpose of these reflections to elaborate an alternative. To mention the following suggestions suffices:

A religious dialogue must first of all be an authentic *dialogue*, without superiority, preconceptions, hidden motives or convictions on either side. What is more, if it is to be an authentic dialogue it must also preclude preconceiving its aims and results. We cannot enter a dialogue having already postulated what will come of it, or having resolved to withdraw should it enter areas we have a priori excluded. Dialogue does not primarily mean study, consultation, examination, preaching, proclamation, learning, etc.; if we insist on dialogue we should respect and follow its rules. Dialogue listens and observes, but it also speaks, corrects and is corrected; it aims at mutual understanding.

Secondly, religious dialogue must be genuinely *religious*, not merely an exchange of doctrines or intellectual opinions. And so it runs the risk of modifying my ideas, my most personal horizons, the very framework of my life. Religious dialogue is not a salon entertainment.

This amounts to saying that dialogue must proceed from the depths of my religious attitude to these same depths in my partner. In other words I understand him, or try to, both from and within my faith, not by putting it aside. How could I possibly comprehend with mere reason something that very often, without necessarily being irrational, claims somehow to be more than sheer rationality?

Imagine we are discussing the meaning and function of

sacrifice. Only if I believe, one way or another, in that act or event that makes sacrifice reasonable shall I be able to understand in depth what my partner really believes, and vice versa of course. Otherwise I may pretend I understand him (because I follow his description and know the effects of sacrifice, etc.), but I shall miss the point of his belief and, in fact, whether I say so or not, most likely regard his belief as pure magic. In brief, the kernel of the purely religious act is phenomenologically undetectable; at least with the theory of phenomenology accepted up to now. I am saying that the *phenomenon* of religion does not exhaust the whole of religious *reality*; so that besides, not opposed to, phenomenology of religion there is yet room for philosophy and theology—and indeed for religion itself.

The peculiar difficulty in the phenomenology of religion is that the religious *pistema* is different from and not reducible to the Husserlian *noema*. The *pistema* is that core of religion which is open or intelligible only to a *religious* phenomenology. In other words, the belief of the believer belongs essentially to the religious phenomenon. There is no 'naked' or 'pure' belief separate from the person who believes. This being the case, the *noema* of a religiously skeptical phenomenologist does not correspond to the *pistema* of the believer. The religious phenomenon appears only as *pistema* and not as mere *noema*. How to reach the *pistema* is an urgent and tantalizing task for religious phenomenology.

We lack a Philosophy of Religion. We have philosophies of religions, i.e., philosophies of particular religious traditions, or we have—and this causes difficulty in the religious encounter—the extrapolation of one religion's philosophy to other religious traditions for which it was neither intended nor suitable.

It almost goes without saying that the Philosophy of Religion I anticipate would not reduce all religions to one homogenous pudding. On the contrary, it would allow the most variegated beliefs and religious traditions to flourish in its field, uprooting only isolationism and misunderstanding (not to say resentment and envy) to make room for a healthy and natural pluralism. We will have a true Philosophy of Religion not by lumping everything together, but by discovering Man's religious root, which grows, flowers and gives fruit in the most multiform way. Only the walls may fall, and private gardens open their gates . . . . Such a philosophy results only from the mystical adventure of seeing truth from within more than one religious tradition. Interreligious dialogue is undoubtedly a preparation for this, a stepping-stone to that intrareligious dialogue where living faith constantly demands from us a total renewal, or—in Christian terms—a real, personal and ever-recurring *metanoia*.

IV. THE CATEGORY OF GROWTH IN COMPARATIVE RELIGION
A Critical Self-examination

ὅς γὰρ οὐκ ἔστιν καθ' ἡμῶν
ὑπὲρ ἡμῶν ἔστιν.
Whoever is not against us,
is for us.

Mk. 9:40 (Lk. 9:50) (+)

+ Significantly enough the Vulgata translated both Mark and Luke: 'Qui enim non est adversus *vos*, pro *vobis* est' probably not wanting to contradict Mt. 12:30 ('Qui non est *mecum* contra *me* est') and Lk. 11:23.

The echo produced by some of my writings dealing with problems in Comparative Religion invites me to restate thematically one of the main issues in the encounter of religions.

This chapter tries to overcome the temptation of self-defense. I shall try to rethink my approach to the problem of the encounter of Christian faith with the religions of the world and present it for correction or even total eclipse. How can I put forward more than a hypothesis in this field of open dialogue just now emerging among religions?

Ultimately my aim is not to defend or attack either Christianity or any other religion, but to understand the problem. It is precisely because I take seriously Christ's affirmation that he is the way, the truth and the life[1] that I cannot reduce his significance only to historical Christianity. It is because I also take seriously the saying of the Gītā that all action done with a good intention reaches Krṣna[2] and the message of the Buddha that he points the way to liberation,[3] that I look for an approach to the encounter of religions that will contain not only a deep respect for but an enlightened confidence in these very traditions—and eventually belief in their messages.

Because I am equally concerned with contemporary Man, only too often wearied by a certain 'religious' inflation when it is a better world for his fellow-beings he wants to build, I cannot consider the meeting of religions exclusively as a problem concerned with the past or relevant only to traditional religions. It speaks to the modern secular Man as well.

1. THE INSUFFICIENT METHODOLOGICAL APPROACHES

One main objection to some of my writings is that I have undertaken a totally 'false method': instead of defending Christianity, showing the demonic character of paganism and 'utilizing' the tools of Hinduism to proclaim the Christian Gospel, I involved myself with 'pagan' absurdities, daring to 'interpret' positively pagan texts in a certain way and thus defending 'paganism' instead of undermining it. The reason for this is alleged to be my assumption that Christ is already present in Hinduism. In short, I 'interpret' paganism with 'Christian concepts', i.e., I misinterpret it, instead of 'utilizing' it for Christian apologetics. Or, in the words of a benevolent Hindu critic, I do just the opposite: My interpretation of Christ is in fact a Hindu interpretation.

But my purpose is not Christian or Hindu apologetics. I am not concerned with defending one or the other religion, one or the other thesis. This does not mean I am betwixt and between and stand nowhere at all; rather I start from the existential situation where I happen to be. I am not assuming the position of the aseptic-scientific mind beyond good and evil or outside the dilemma that claims to be ultimate. I affirm only that I am starting from my personal situation without caring at this moment to describe it further. I am not writing on behalf of one or another religious tradition. I am speaking for myself and inviting my contemporaries to sincere dialogue.

Now, and this has been sometimes a cause of misunderstanding, I cannot speak many languages at the same time or defend many fronts simultaneously. External circumstances have led me to write more often for Christians—trying to open them up to other religious intuitions—than for Hindus or Buddhists. Some, contrary to the criticism voiced above, consider this a 'proof' that I am still on the Christian side. Others have interpreted this in the opposite way, namely that I believe Christians are in more urgent need of that opening to others than Hindus and Buddhists. Again, I am not defending myself, but simply trying to understand.

It seems to me that my deepest divergence from some of my critics is not so much in method as in understanding the fundamental Christian fact. Ultimately I would not accept absolutizing Christianity in order to consider that its truth has an exclusive claim that monopolizes salvation. In other words, I would not equate historical Christianity with transhistorical truth; nor, for that matter, ahistorical Hinduism with a historical message. Insofar as it is a historical religion, Christianity belongs to history and should not transgress the boundaries of history; insofar as it conveys ahistorical values, Hinduism should not be totally identified with a historical religion. I am well aware, of course, that Christianity contains more than just a historical message, that the history of salvation implies the salvation of history and that this latter has an eschatological value transcending history. I am convinced, similarly, that Hinduism is also a historical phenomenon and a cultural asset in the history of mankind. Most of the misunderstandings in this field arise from the fact that only too often comparisons are made between heterogeneous elements: We judge one religious tradition from inside and the other from outside. Any vision from within, with belief and personal commitment, includes at once the concreteness (and so the limitations) of that particular religion and the universal truth it embodies. A view from outside cannot see this link and judges only by objectified values. But religion, by definition—that is, as what it claims to be—is not completely objectifiable, nor is it reducible to mere subjectivity.

For this reason I do not accept the *utilization-interpretation* dilemma, nor do I find that these approaches do justice to the dialogue among religions toward which we are today impelled.

The difference between an exposition of Christian mysteries *utilizing* Indian or other concepts and images on the one hand, and an *interpretation* of the religions of the world by means of Christian concepts on the other, would be important were I engaged in the defense of a particular doctrine. But for one who sincerely strives to find and express the truth, for one who does not discard either Hindu or Christian tradition as demonic, the difference is not relevant. Indeed, someone who humbly desires to make a radical investigation cannot take as his starting point a position that fundamentally and inexorably begs the question. I do not think either Christian or Hindu has to start with a kind of entrenched a priori that makes any meeting and dialogue impossible from the outset.

I am not considering whether or not what Christ conveyed is the same message Hinduism conveys. I am, however, making a fundamental assumption. The *ultimate* religious *fact* does not lie in the realm of doctrine or even individual self-consciousness. Therefore it can—and may well—be present everywhere and in every religion, although its 'explicitation' may require varied degrees of discovery, realization, evangelization, revelation, hermeneutics, etc. And this makes it plausible that this fundamental—religious—*fact* may have different names, interpretations, levels of consciousness and the like, which are not irrelevant but which may be existentially equivalent for the person undergoing the concrete process of realization.

In a word, I am pleading for the *dekerygmatization* of faith. The kerygma—like the myth—has its place within any religion, but the 'proclamation of the message' should not be identified without qualifications with the reality religions aim to disclose. I would apply this in a very special way to Christianity and I may also say my reason for this is a conviction that the living and ultimately the real Christ is not the kerygma of the Lord, but the Lord himself. The naked Christ means also the 'dekerygmatized' Christ.

I would say there is a primordial theandric fact that appears with a certain fullness in Jesus,[4] but that is equally manifested and at work elsewhere. This is the Mystery that exists since the beginning of time and will appear only at the end of time in its 'capital' fullness.[5] It is in my opinion a disheartening 'microdoxy' to monopolize that mystery and make it the private property of Christians.

The main different between 'interpretation' and 'utilization' then seems to lie in this:

The *utilization* of, say, Greek or Hindu concepts to expound Christian doctrine implies that I know well what Christian belief is and that I *use* some thought-patterns from an external source to expound Christian doctrine.

The *interpretation* of, say, Hinduism or Greek religion, along Christian lines, implies that I know well what Hinduism and Greek religion is and that I interpose some thought patterns coming from an external source (Christianity) in order to explain those very religions.

Let us now analyze these two methodological approaches to the encounter of religions, *utilization* and *interpretation*. It is my contention that these two methods are not valid methods for a fruitful encounter of religions. Moreover, they seem to be incompatible with at least a significant part of the Christian attitude. Further, I shall contend that only the category of growth does justice to the real religious situation of our time.

a. Utilization

Time and again it is said that the proper Christian attitude in the encounter of religions is that demonstrated by the Christian Fathers themselves: *utilizing* the elements of pre-Christian thought to expound Christian doctrine. Undoubtedly this has been an opinion held by Christians and by people of other religions as well.

To begin with, historical evidence for the first generation of Christians utilizing already-existing elements of thought merely to express their own Christian ideas as their main or only procedure is very questionable. And, although this may sometimes have been the method, it was never the creative nor the prevailing attitude in Christianity. History shows that precisely where the Christian message succeeded in transforming a society it was never by such a 'utilization', but, on the contrary, by its being assimilated—the Christian word is incarnated—by that particular religion and culture: the Christian fact being the leaven.

Very often indeed, we cannot say whether the Fathers of the Church were 'utilizing', or just the opposite, and in fact much of the polemics and tension in the Patristic period is due precisely to the coexistence of both processes: that of 'utilizing' and that of being utilized. Were Plato's ideas Christianized or was Christianity 'Platonized'? Were Aristotle's concepts of *ousia* and the like utilized for the Christian doctrine of the Trinity, or did the Christian idea of the Trinity evolve as it did due to the internal dialectic of the concepts thus introduced? To put it differently, is not a great part of what is today called Christian doctrine or even Christianity precisely the result of such a symbiosis?

'Christian doctrine' did not come out of nothing, but was the expression of certain beliefs within a specific thought-pattern, which, in the beginning, was either 'Jewish' or 'Gentile' (this word embracing more than one cultural form), but certainly not Christian. No Christian doctrine of the Trinity nor any Christology existed before its expression in Gentile or Jewish categories. The Christian experience—belief or whatever one wishes to call it, but assuredly not doctrine—was moulded, found expression—in a word, became doctrine— by means of already existing thought-patterns. It could not be otherwise. The first Christians did not 'utilize' Greek or other thought-categories of the times in order to convey what had not yet found expression. On the contrary, only by means of these categories—Jewish and Gentile—could the Christian experience be expressed and understood at all. A cogent proof for it is the significant fact that orthodox and heretical views in the Trinitarian and Christological controversies of that age both used the terminology of their respective milieux. Thus, to say 'three *ousiai*' or 'three *hypostases*' (substances) meant one thing to Origen and another to Arius, or to say 'three *prosopa*' (persons) meant one thing to Hippolytus and another to Sabellius. They were not utilizing Greek concepts to express one single Christian intuition, but they had a different understanding of the Christian fact, perhaps because they were carried away by the very concepts they used. One could almost say they were utilized, used by those very concepts.

In fact, Greek concepts handled (and often mishandled) the Christian event. Saint John, for instance, did not utilize

(and transform) the Philonic concept of *logos* to convey his
'message'; it was almost the other way around: the *logos* took
flesh, I would say—begging not to be misunderstood—not
only in the womb of Mary, but also in the midst of the intellectual speculation on the *logos* at that time. To use utterly
new words and expressions to say what Christ was all about
would have been unintelligible—and impossible. To give expression to the Christian faith not by dint of willful and calcu-
lated utilization but through a natural, cultural and spiritual
process, the only possibility was—and always is—to let it take
form, name and flesh in terms of the contemporary culture. In
scholastic terms: The logical analogy of the concepts, necessary for their intelligibility outside their univocal realm, implies also an ontological analogy. If the Johannine concept of
logos were not somehow analogous to the pre-Christian concept, if it did not start from an interpretation of a concept
already existing, it could neither be intelligible nor in any way
'inspired'. A parallel example would be that of the Buddha
interpreting the already-existing concept of *nirvāṇa* in a new
and original way.

But one may retort that the situation is different today:
There *are* dogmas, there *is* a Church. There is now a definite
Christian doctrine and even a so-called 'Christian thought'.
But, it is further said, such 'thought' can very well profit from
concepts and ideas borrowed from other cultures and religions. This we may grant for the sake of the argument, but we
should emphasize that such a method of borrowing will never
go very deep nor lead us very far; it will touch only the surface
and lead to an artificial and decidedly shallow adaptation.
There will emerge from it neither synthesis nor symbiosis, nor
even a serious confrontation. It will all remain foreign and
external, mere superstructure.

That there is now an elaborate Christian thought-system
makes it all the more urgent to overcome the danger of isolation and self-satisfaction by reaching out to meet other religious traditions, learning from them and interpreting them in
the light of one's own beliefs. Two main reasons seem relevant

here. The first is the almost self-evident fact that the Western Christian tradition seems to be exhausted, I might almost say effete, when it tries to express the Christian message in a meaningful way for our times. Only by cross-fertilization and mutual fecundation may the present state of affairs be overcome; only by stepping over present cultural and philosophical boundaries can Christian life again become creative and dynamic. Obviously this applies to the other religions as well: It is a two-way traffic. The encounter of religions today is vital for the religious life of contemporary Man; otherwise, traditional religions will remain altogether obsolete, irrelevant relics of the past, and what is worse, modern Man will be uprooted and impoverished.

The time for one-way traffic in the meeting of cultures and religions is, at least theoretically, over, and if there are still powerful vestiges of a past colonialistic attitude, they are dying out by the very fact that they become conscious. Neither monologue nor conquest is tenable. The *spolia aegyptiorum* mentality is today no longer possible nor in any way justifiable. To think that one people, one culture, one religion has the right—or the duty for that matter—to dominate all the rest belongs to a past period in world history. Our contemporary degree of consciousness and our present-day conscience, East and West, finds, by and large, such a pretension utterly untenable. The meeting point is neither my house nor the mansion of my neighbor, but the crossroads outside the walls, where we may eventually decide to put up a tent—for the time being.[6]

Finally, there is a theoretical point to consider: If the use of a concept foreign to a given cultural setup is to be made viable, if it is to be successfully grafted onto another system of thought (the Christian for example), it will succeed because it has somehow attained a certain homogeneity with the host cultural and religious world so that it may live there. If this is the case, it amounts to recognizing that its possible use depends on a certain previous homogeneity, on a certain presence of the one meaning within the other framework; otherwise it would be completely impossible to utilize the concept in question. In spite of the heterogeneity between the Greek and Christian conception of the *logos*, for instance, the former had to offer a certain affinity with the new meaning that would be enhanced once it was assumed. In other words, 'utilization', even if it is admitted as a proper procedure, can be fruitful only if based on a previous relatedness that is the condition for its use. Only homogeneous materials can be used if any integration is to survive. The real problem, thus, lies deeper—and elsewhere.

b. Interpretation

Some critics maintain that it is quite wrong in the encounter of religions (at least from the Christian point of view) to interpret the texts and statements of other religious traditions in light of the Christian intuition.

If the faith of the Christian were totally foreign to such traditions, if the Christian fact had nothing to do with the fundamental religious fact or human reality in its ultimate concern, then obviously to introduce a hermeneutical principle (the Christian one) completely alien to those traditions would be unwarranted. But this is not necessarily a Christian position.

Be this as it may, I would offer the following condensed remarks.

First, one could also question here the historical accuracy of the statement that authentic Christians never interpreted pre-Christian religions but only utilized them for their own kerygma. I wonder then, what it was Saint Paul did with the Jewish Bible if not interpret it, and rather drastically at that. Moreover, most of the Church Fathers and the Scholastics undoubtedly did this very thing vis-à-vis 'non-Christian' thinkers and Greek concepts, i.e., they interpreted them according to what they thought to be the Christian line of development. In this way the traditional doctrine of the *sensus plenior* was developed: the fuller meaning of pre-Christian ideas seen in the light of Christ. This idea underlies nothing less than the incorporation of the Old Testament into Christianity.

Secondly, the question becomes even clearer if we consider that ultimately we cannot use a concept without at the same time interpreting it in a certain way. If Saint Paul, for instance, had 'utilized' a Stoic or Gnostic concept of *soma* (body) without interpreting it in his own way, this would have amounted to accepting fully its Stoic or Gnostic connotations. The work of polishing, or emphasizing, or even sometimes twisting, which theologians of every age have always done: What is this if not simply interpreting or, I would say, reinterpreting already existing concepts?

Third, the main objection to a Christian interpretation of the religions of the world seems to rest on a double assumption: on the idea that all that does not belong 'officially' and 'visibly' to historical Christianity, or to the Church, is sin and satanic (an extrapolation of the saying that everything not born of God is sin[7]) and on the fear that such an interpretation would mean recognizing that the Spirit of God has also been at work in other religious traditions[8] and that even Christ, who is before Abraham,[9] is somehow present and effective in those other religions. (Lord, we have seen some performing miracles in your name who do not belong to our group. . . .[10] 'The rock indeed was Christ!'[11])

I personally cannot subscribe to any opinion that monopolizes God, *logos*, Christ and even Jesus and sets the rules for how the kingdom of God must work. I disagree from a purely human standpoint, as well as from scientific, theological and Christian points of view. There were zealots even among the Apostles, but Christ was not a zealot.

Finally, there remains the objection from the other side, i.e., from the followers of other religious traditions. Are they going to be satisfied with a Christian interpretation?

One may answer, first of all, that these religions are going to be satisfied even less by the other method, which simply uses their own tools to preach something apparently contrary to their traditions and beliefs. Yet the force of the argument clearly does not come from this quarter.

The one reason underlying resistance to a Christian interpretation seems to be that, with few exceptions, Christ has been considered the monopoly of Christians, as if Christ were *ad usum delphini*, solely for the benefit of orthodox believers. And so when one mentions even the name of Christ, other religions understand it in a polemical or at least foreign way.

Now, it is clear that any genuine 'Christian' interpretation must be valid and true, and for this very reason it must also be acceptable to those who are being interpreted; a basic methodological rule for any interpretation. This means that no interpretation of any religion is valid if the followers of that religion do not recognize it as such. But this means also, by the same token, that nobody can propose as Christian something that Christians do not recognize as such. On the other hand the history of religious traditions is not closed and it shows that certain ideas or conceptions denounced as heretical at a given moment were accepted later on. In point of fact the evolution—and, as I am going to say, the growth—of any religion has been mainly brought about by 'foreign' ideas incorporated into the body of beliefs.

Further, there is still another, though ambivalent, reason for the 'Christian interpretation' or any interpretation of one religion by another, for that matter. I may point out the pro and the contra.

Pro. If the Christian interpretation of, say, *karma* is to be a valid one, as has already been said, it has to be valid for the two traditions. This is to say that such an interpretation will have to have reached a depth where the one tradition does not find it deformed and the other one finds it acceptable. Obviously the new interpretation may find some shades of meaning because of its incorporation into Christianity that Hindus and Buddhists may not accept; but provided they recognize the starting interpretation as a legitimate one, nothing stands in the way for the new step.

Contra. Religions are organic wholes and each particular tenet makes sense within the entire body of doctrine. Now to transplant one particular notion into another body is not only a delicate operation, it also requires a homogeneous body to receive it. Otherwise what we have done is to get stimulated by the 'foreign' tenet, but in fact we have not crossed the boundaries of one tradition. This is particularly visible with the very words we use. Words are meaningful within a context and mere translation may not do. In other terms, not everything is susceptible of an exogenous interpretation.

Here we must confess that a great deal of fundamental work has still to be done. I would like now to state tentatively the direction in which I would be inclined to look for further research.

2. PHILOSOPHIES AND PHILOSOPHY OF RELIGION

One fact should be clearly and sincerely acknowledged: Considering the geographical and historical coordinates of our times, we do not have a Philosophy of Religion worthy of the name. What is termed philosophy of religion is usually a particular philosophy of a particular religion expressed in more or less vague or universal terms and then applied almost a priori to all other 'religions' of the world. Undoubtedly mankind can be considered a unity, and from the reflection of a particular group one may sometimes draw conclusions valid for the entire human race, but this approximate method is distinctly insufficient as a working and effective Philosophy of Religion for our times. Even if in the past such efforts were made, the world view that prompted such attempts has been superseded today when the whole earth—for good or ill—begins to form a geographical and historical unit for the first time in human existence.

The fact that traditional religions are mainly oriented to the past, for instance, and that the religious vitality of mankind has produced new forms of religiousness marginal to, if not in conflict with, traditional religions is part of the same problem: namely, we do not have a Philosophy of Religion. Ideologies and other secular forms that claim a total hold on the human person, and thereby the right to direct his life, are numberless in our times. Morphologically, in fact, they are religions, but few would so call themselves because the very name has fallen into widespread disrepute.

Our main point follows. We may easily agree that one

cannot envision even the possibility of a Philosophy of Religion without the internal experience peculiar to religion. In terms of classical Christian scholasticism, theology is a *charisma,* and faith is required for a real and creative theologian. And here the philosophical and the theological activity should not be artificially severed.

Now, in spite of the claim of every religion to touch the very core of the human being, the 'experience of religion' does not exist. What is given is a religious experience within one particular context, or we may also grant that there is a peculiar internal experience of or within *a* particular religion. Religion in general does not exist.

This would justify *a* philosophy of *a* religion, but not Philosophy of Religion. Either then we agree it is possible internally and authentically to experience more than one religion or we renounce forever a Philosophy of Religion valid for the different world religions; or else, as is generally the case today, Philosophy of Religion is merely replaced by phenomenology of religions—and even then the problem is not solved, as we shall see in the following chapter.

We in no way belittle phenomenology of religion, which has earned much merit in recent times; but to consider it a substitute for Philosophy of Religion would be a serious mistake. *Suum cuique.*

I am not maintaining here that no Philosophy of Religion is possible without the specific 'theological' *charisma* in the scholastic sense. Whatever conception of philosophy (or theology if we prefer) we may have, only a philosophy or theology of religion that takes into account the facts, categories and intuitions of a particular religion is able and entitled to handle the phenomena of that religion. But for this we must know such data not merely by hearsay but through a genuine effort to understand. Even the strictest philosophical positivism is no exception to this. If, as this latter will tell us, Philosophy of Religion is only the scientific analysis of religious language, one must nevertheless know the particular language, which originated from assumptions rather different, perhaps, than the language of the positivist philosopher himself. In brief, it is not only a question of proper translation; we need a common symbolics not only to check the translation and establish two-way communication, but also even to make the translation. In order to say 'table' means 'Tisch' I need another common term of reference (my finger, my eyes, etc.) able to transfer (translate) the meaning.

Philosophy of Religion is only made possible by a prior philosophy of religions. Only after this, which is more than just a digest of philosophies of religions, will we be on the way to a Philosophy of Religion capable of fulfilling the task that falls to such a discipline today. To elaborate a Philosophy of Religion we need to take religions seriously and, further, to experience them from within, to believe, in one way or another, in what these religions say. Otherwise, we remain floating on the surface. To know what a religion says, we must understand what it says, but for this we must somehow believe in what it says. Religions are not purely objectifiable data; they are also and essentially personal, subjective. As we have said, the particular belief of the believer belongs essentially to religion. Without that belief no philosophy of religions is possible. To merely describe the tenets or practices the followers of a particular religion claim to acknowledge is not yet philosophy of religions, much less Philosophy of Religion. Needless to say this is only a necessary precondition or requirement, insufficient by itself for a critical Philosophy of Religion.

This seems to be a major challenge in our times; lacking an authentic Philosophy of Religion we shall be able to understand neither the different world religions nor the people and cultures of this earth, for religion is the soul of a culture and one of the most important factors in shaping the human character individually and collectively. Undoubtedly the extrapolation of a particular philosophy into fields beyond the scope of its original application is no longer justifiable.

Yet in fact this still happens in many philosophical, theological and religious quarters. Christianity is perhaps the religion that has been most concerned with the problem, and yet not only does it not possess any Philosophy of Religion, but it continues to extrapolate all unawares. When, for instance, Saint Paul speaks about the Gentiles or the idolators, he has in mind the people of Corinth or Asia Minor or those whom he considers for whatever reason to warrant the name. To apply the Jew-Gentile dichotomy outside its sphere and call 'gentile' the Hindus, Buddhists (and even, for that matter, Muslims!) is an unwarranted extrapolation, to say the least. Biblical scholarship today does not insist that the entire planet was under water in Noah's time or in utter darkness at the Crucifixion of Christ. It has set geographical boundaries to those statements, but it still has not sufficiently examined the anthropological, metaphysical and religious boundaries of the Old and New Testaments.

Is such an enterprise, a Philosophy of Religion possible? I believe it cannot be affirmed a priori that it is impossible, although it may remain only an ideal. Philosophy can encompass more than one religion because one can have an authentic internal religious experience in more than one religious tradition without betraying any of them, and of course without confusing genuine experience with artificial experiment. One cannot experiment with religions as if they were rats or plants, but one can believe in them as authentic paths and try to understand and eventually to integrate more than one religious tradition. After all, most of mankind's great religious geniuses did not create or found new forms of religiousness out of nothing; rather they fused more than one religious stream, moulding them with their own prophetic gifts. But one need not be a prophet or a founder of a religion to be creative in this new field of research; the philosopher of religion needs, however, to be a believer and to be sufficiently humble and ready to undergo with his faith not an experiment but an experience.

I have said that a philosophy of religion is not impossible, but should have added immediately one condition. And this condition links us again with the traditional philosophical or theological activity in contradistinction to the individualistic character of Western modernity. This condition is, in old parlance, the scholastic (in sense of school), corporate or ecclesial character of the philosophical enterprise. In present-day terms we may prefer to speak of the dialogical character of Philosophy of Religion.

A genuine Philosophy of Religion in our times, if it is to maintain the claim to speak about the religious dimension of Man, has to be critically aware that no single individual nor any single religious tradition has access to the universal range of the human experience. It must needs then pull together the findings, experiences and data coming from the four directions of the earth: It has to be dialogical and like a net encompass the different religious experiences of mankind.

The main thing favoring such an enterprise is not the individual's psychological capacity to sincerely experience more than one religious tradition, but the fact that there exists something like a fundamental religiousness, a constitutive religious dimension in Man, an inbuilt religious or basically human factor, whatever we may care to call it. Surely no religious tradition today takes such hold of the entire human being that it leaves no room for communication and dialogue. Man indeed transcends historical and cultural boundaries.

Mankind—human nature if one prefers, is meta-ontologically one. This allows the possibility of an experience that certainly implies overcoming the actual boundaries of a particular religion, without its betrayal.

3. THE VITAL ISSUE: GROWTH

Earlier we said neither the *use* of a foreign tradition to enrich another one nor the *interpretation* of one religion in the light of another is adequate or appropriate to the philosophical task and the religious need of our times. I submit that the one category able to carry the main burden in the religious encounter and in the further development of religion (and religions) is *growth*. Theology or philosophy, and religion even more, are not simply matters of archaeological interest, nor is religion mainly directed to the past. On the contrary, the future, hope, eschatology, the end of Man, life and the world are fundamental religious categories. Religion is equally inclined towards the future, full of that *epektasis* of the Greek Christian Patristic writings, i.e., that attitude of more than expectation, of constantly leaning towards the trans- or super-human end of Man. In the life of religion as in the life of a person, where there is no growth there is decay; to stop is stagnation and death.

It would be wrong and methodologically false to restrict the theological task to just imitating the elders. Obviously it is a risky adventure to start towards the *terra incognita* of a really new land in religious consciousness and proceed by discovering new paths. 'Men of Galilee, what are you doing here just gazing at the skies . . .?'[12]

After much effort and many painful misunderstandings, Christian theology has accepted as fact what in certain theological circles is called the development of dogma. This seems to be a good starting point, but it would hardly suffice if interpreted merely as a kind of explication of something already there. Were religious consciousness static, our task would be only to unfold what was already there nicely 'folded'. There is, however, undoubtedly a development in religious consciousness. Two points should be made immediately in this connection. First, religious consciousness is something more than an external development of a knowing organ that at a certain moment discovers something of which it was not previously aware. And, since religious consciousness is an essential part of religion itself, the development of this consciousness means the development of religion itself. Secondly, it amounts to more than just a development in personal consciousness; at the very least human consciousness is set in evolution. What develops, in fact, is the entire cosmos, all creation, reality. The whole universe expands. In a word, there is real growth in Man, in the World and, I would also add, in God, at least inasmuch as neither immutability nor change are categories of the divine. The divinity is constant newness, pure act as the scholastics said.

So there is not only a development of dogma, there is also a real development of consciousness: of Man and of all reality. We may—or may not—have a system of thought sufficiently elaborated to express this fact adequately, but it is one thing to endure the limitation of the human mind struggling to find proper expression and another thing to dismiss an intuition because it is still in the throes of birth, still a *concipiendum* and not yet a *conceptum*. After all, what is born into life here on earth already complete? Only something already dead, stillborn. As is often remarked, only dead languages do not tolerate mistakes (nobody left to accept them), but a living language has ample place for today's mistakes, which may become tomorrow's rule. The physical theory of an expanding universe may furnish a fair image of what happens in the ontological realm as well.

Without allowing for such growth, no religious maturity is possible. But here growth does not mean only linear development. In spite of every Christian theological contrivance, the Jewish point of view is quite right when it judges not only Paul but Christ too as real innovators. Given this perspective, the members of the Sanhedrin were not so wrong in condemning Jesus. They really understood what it was all about: not merely evolution, reform or improvement, but a real mutation, a new step, another sphere, more akin to revolution than to evolution. It is almost a platitude to say that if Jesus were to come to earth now, the Christian Church would put him to death. I interpret this not to mean that the Church has betrayed the message of Jesus (this is not my point now), but that Christ would introduce another revolution, another step, a new wine that he would not allow to be poured into old skins.[13] This constant growth should be a fundamental element of sacramental theology, especially of the liturgical Eucharist.

Growth is perhaps the most pertinent category to express this situation, which is more than simple development or explication. In growth there is continuity as well as novelty, development as well as a real assimilation of something that was outside and is now incorporated, made one body. In growth, there is freedom. Perhaps nowhere else is human freedom more visible and more magnificent than in the consciousness of the religious person who discovers that he or she is the co-creator, the shaper and builder not only of his or her own life but also of the life of the cosmos: Man is the artist of the mystical body, the free agent who may let himself and the world go one way or another, who may lead history in one or another direction. Nothing is more fascinating than the religious existence seen and lived as such a dynamism.

I repeat: Growth means continuity and development, but it also implies transformation and revolution. Growth does not exclude mutation; on the contrary, there are moments even in the biological realm when only a real mutation can account for further life. We know roughly the law of growth for a plant or for a child's body; we do not know, and in a way we cannot know, the ways growth may possibly grow further. The future is not just a repetition of the past. (I hope one result of Man's landing on the moon will be to liberate us from provincial horizons and foreshortened views.) How Hinduism needs to grow or how Christianity or modern Humanism has to grow we may not yet know. The prophet's function is not precisely to know in advance but to point out the direction and to go ahead, to ascend the ladder of time, space and the spirit. There are false prophets, indeed, but for the same reason that there is false silver and not, so far, false earth or water; we only falsify things worth falsifying.

Growth does not exclude rupture and internal or external revolution. We know what the growth of an adolescent means only once the evolution is complete. We do not know where we are going. Yet in this common ignorance genuinely religious people experience real fellowship and fraternal communion.

Growth does not deny a process of death and resurrection; quite the contrary. If growth is to be genuine and not merely a cancer, it implies a negative as well as a positive metabolism, death as well as a new life. That we must constantly kill the idols that creep in from all sides, this we are prepared to accept; we also know that the prophets' lot is to be crushed between the temple and the palace. It seems, at least to me, an empirical truth that *metanoia* is the first condition for sound growth and real life.

But what about Islam, Hinduism, Christianity? I am tempted to give the answer Jesus gave to a similar question put by Peter: 'If it should be my will that he wait until I come, what is that to you? You follow me!'[14]

In the contemporary scene where everything is in the fires of revision and reform, in which every value is contested and the *metanoia* almost total, the authentically religious Man cannot shut himself off, close his ears and eyes, and simply gaze toward heaven or brood over the past; he cannot ignore his fellow-Men and act as if religion has assured him he has no more to learn, nothing to change. He must throw himself into the sea and begin to walk, even if his feet falter and his heart fails.[15] Who are we to stifle the growing seed, to choke humble and personal buds, to quench the smoking wick?[16]

4. BIBLIOGRAPHICAL NOTE

Besides the more than one hundred book reviews scattered among specialized journals and the discussion that took place (over a period of several years) in the Bombay Weekly *The Examiner* (from 1965 onwards), cf.:

D. Reetz, 'Raymond Panikkar's Theology of Religion', *Religion and Society* (Bangalore, September, 1968), XV:3, pp. 32-54; D.C. Mulder, 'Raymond Panikkar's Dialog Met Het Hindoeïsme', *Gereformeers Theologisch Tiydschrift* (August, 1969), pp. 186-198; and F. Molinario, 'L'evangelizzazione della cultura e delle religione nella sperienza e negli scritti di R. Panikkar', *Testimonianza* (No. 144, 1972).

Regarding specific points, cf. the author's answers to:

J.A. Cuttat, 'Vergeistigungs "Technik" und Umgestaltung in Christus', *Kairos* (Salzburg, 1/1959), pp. 18-30; P. Hacker, 'Magie, Gott, Person und Gnade in Hinduismus', *Kairos* (Salzburg, 4/1960), pp. 225-233; and K. Rudolph, 'Die Problematik der Religionswissenschaft als akademisches Lehrfach', *Kairos* (Salzburg, 1/1967), pp. 22-42 (all of which may be found in *Kairos* [Salzburg, 1/1960], pp. 45-45; [2/1961], pp. 112-114; and [1/1968], pp. 56-67 respectively).

As for the negative criticism these pages have tried to meet without polemics, cf. the article-review by P. Hacker of the author's *Kultmysterium in Hinduismus und Christentum* in *Theologische Revue,* nr. 6 (1967), pp. 370-378, and also Hacker's short essay 'Interpretation und "Benutzung"', 'Kleine Beitrage' in *Zeitschrift für Missionswissenschaft und Religionswissenschaft,* Inhalt des 51 (Juli 1967), heft 3, pp. 259-263.

NOTES

1. Cf. Jn. 14:6.
2. Cf. BG IX, 26-34.
3. Cf. Saṁyutta-nikāya V, 421-423.
4. Col. 1:19.
5. Cf. 1 Cor. 2:7; Eph. 1:9-10.
6. Cf. Mk. 9:5.
7. Cf. Rom. 14:23.
8. Rom. 10:10.
9. Jn. 8:58.
10. Lk. 9:49; Mk. 9:38.
11. 1 Cor. 10:4.
12. Acts 1:11.
13. Lk. 5:37-38.
14. Jn. 21:22.
15. Mt. 14:28 sq.
16. Mt. 12:20; cf. Is. 42:3.

V. ŚŪNYATĀ AND PLĒRŌMA
The Buddhist and Christian Response to the Human Predicament

pūrṇasya pūrṇam ādāya
pūrṇam evāvaśiṣyate
Subtracting fullness from fullness
still fullness remains.

Upaniṣadic Invocation (+)

+ Cf. BU V, 1.

1. THE HUMAN PREDICAMENT

In spite of the scores of attempts at defining religion I may venture this simple and brief statement: Religion is the path Man follows in order to reach the purpose of life, or, shorter, religion is the *way of salvation*. One has to add immediately that here the words 'way' and 'salvation' do not claim any specific content; rather they stand for the existential pilgrimage Man undertakes in the belief that this enterprise will help him achieve the final purpose or end of life.[1] A *way to fulfillment*—if we prefer.

In other words, under the particular perspective that we may call religion, every human culture presents three elements: (1) a vision of Man as he actually appears to be *(hic et nunc)*, (2) a certain more or less developed notion of the end or final station of Man *(illic et postea)*, and (3) the means for going from the former situation to the latter.[2]

The first element may be called the *human predicament*, i.e., the particular view of how Man is seen and evaluated. I use this expression rather than the more common 'human condition' in order to stress that not all religions view Man's factual situation along the lines 'condition' suggests. Man is not independent of what he takes himself to be and the human condition is precisely conditioned by Man's own view of it. By human predicament I mean the factual status of Man as it is evaluated in a particular conception forming part of that factual status itself.

No religion, and much less those we shall consider, can be

encompassed in a monolithic doctrine, as if a single doctrine could sum up all it stands for. This chapter will choose only a pair of notions, one from each tradition, to represent an orthodox view in the respective religions.

The human predicament seen by the Buddhist tradition could be summarized: (1) in a philosophical presupposition, the *anatmavāda*;[3] (2) in a theological statement, the *āryasatyāni*,[4] which expands the anthropocosmic intuition of *sarva duḥkha*;[5] and (3) in a moral injunction best rendered by the last words of the Buddha: 'Work out your salvation with diligence.'[6]

The human predicament seen by the Christian tradition could be summarized: (1) in a philosophical presupposition, the creation of the world;[7] (2) in a theological statement, the redeeming or saving power of Christ,[8] which expands the cosmotheandric intuition of the incarnation;[9] and (3) in a moral injunction best rendered by the words of Christ summing up the Law and the Prophets: 'You shall love the Lord your God with all your heart, and all your soul, and all your might. . . .'[10] You shall love your neighbor as yourself.'[11]

We may try to express in our own words the gist of this double vision. It should be remembered that until recently these two traditions agreed about the human predicament. Rightly or wrongly, they seem to concur in saying that Man is endowed with a craving—literally a thirst[12]—or with a lust—literally a desire[13]—that is the cause of his unhappiness. The two religions will elaborate this as an Ignorance or a Fall, so that enlightenment or redemption is required to overcome the human predicament. In any case the human predicament is neither as it should be nor as it could be. The Buddha[14] and the Christ[15] claim to remedy this situation. Man has to transcend his present condition in order to be freed, i.e., disentangled from the wheel of *saṁsāra*,[16] from this *kosmos*.[17] Both Buddhism and Christianity stand for human liberation.[18]

And here both traditions express an almost universal human experience. Both are convinced that Man is a being not yet finished, a reality unachieved, growing, becoming, on the way, a pilgrim. This is the human predicament. The real problem lies in the response these two world religions give to it.

2. THE BUDDHIST AND CHRISTIAN RESPONSES

a. Nirvāṇa and Sōtēria

As we have said, the second element of all religions is the notion that there is an end or a final station of Man. Man, this unfinished being, is not to remain as he is but has to undergo a more or less radical transformation, a change, in order to reach that state which Buddhism calls nirvāṇa[19] and Christianity sōtēria.[20] Religion is the dynamism toward a terminus ad quem, originating in a disconformity with the status quo.

Significantly enough, the canonical writings of both traditions do not seem inclined to limit the nature of these two terms. Nirvāṇa is simply the cessation of becoming,[21] of all saṁskāras,[22] of all links,[23] of every thirst.[24] It is the blowing out of all the karmas,[25] the indescribable term of which not even being can be predicated,[26] the radical originating power of everything,[27] and the end with neither way in nor out.[28] It is beyond all dialectic[29] and thinking,[30] without subject or object.[31] The whole effort lies in reaching it, not in describing or understanding it.[32] But this sentence is false if it is taken to link nirvāṇa in any way with our will or imagination.[33] Nirvāṇa is 'unborn, unbecome, unmade, unaggregated'.[34] Nirvāṇa is not transcendent in the usual sense of the word; were it to transcend anything, it would already be transcendentally linked with what it transcends.[35] Nirvāṇa is the mere destruction or rather the unmaking[36] of all that is and that, by the very fact that it can be undone, destroyed and negated, proves its nonreality, so that nirvāṇa is the most positive 'thing' because it destroys nothingness.

The same vagueness seems to mark the Christian scriptural idea of sōtēria. It is salvation from perdition,[37] from death,[38] through Christ,[39] who leads to salvation.[40] It seems to be eternal[41] for it is the salvation of our lives.[42] Often salvation is used without further qualification, in apparent acceptance of common usage.[43] There is a way,[44] a word,[45] and a knowledge[46] of salvation. Jesus is the savior,[47] he saves the people from their sins,[48] and there is salvation in no one else.[49]

In other words, neither *nirvāṇa* nor *sōtēria* has developed cosmological or metaphysical underpinnings. *Nirvāṇa* is the extinction of the human condition and *sōtēria* the freeing from sin.

b. Śūnyatā and Plērōma

It would require an entire volume to render even cursorily the different interpretations of these central notions. As already indicated, we shall alleviate the difficulty by choosing two significant examples and offering only the bare sketch of their doctrines. The two key words here are *śūnyatā*[50] and *plērōma*,[51] emptiness and fullness. Both are radical and both could be said to represent most emphatically the quintessence of their respective traditions. Furthermore, as the prima facie meaning of the words themselves suggests, both terms seem to be at total variance, not only with one another, but also with modern Humanistic traditions.

The end of the journey, the goal of Man is by definition *nirvāṇa* or *sōtēria*, but the nature of this goal is supposed to be *śūnyatā* in the former case and *plērōma* in the latter, according to some schools in the respective traditions.

In complete harmony with the central Buddhist intuition of *nairātmyavāda*, or the doctrine of the ultimate unsubstantiality of all things, the concept of *śūnyatā* (vacuity, voidness, emptiness) tries to express the very essence of the absolute, the ultimate nature or reality of all things.[52]

Śūnyavāda is not philosophical nihilism or metaphysical agnosticism, but a positive and concrete affirmation, one of the deepest human intuitions regarding the ultimate structure of reality.[53] It says that everything, absolutely everything, that falls under the range of our experience—actual or possible—is void of that (superimposed and thus only falsely appearing) consistency with which we tend to embellish our contingency.

All, including our reason with which we express this very idea, is in the grip of contingent flux. The 'other shore' in the recurring Buddhist metaphor is so totally transcendent that it does not exist; the very thought of it mystifies and negates it.[54] 'Nirvāṇa is saṃsāra and saṃsāra is nirvāṇa', says one well-known formulation,[55] repeated again and again in different forms.[56] There is no way to go to the other shore because there is no bridge, nor even another shore. This recognition is the highest wisdom, the *advaitic* or nondualistic intuition or the *prajñāpāramitā*. To recognize saṃsāra as saṃsāra, i.e., as the flux of existence and that same existence as being in flux, is already the beginning of enlightenment, not because one transcends it (for there is no 'other place' behind or beyond) but because this very recognition sweeps away the veil of ignorance that consists precisely in taking as real or substantial that which is only pure void and vacuity.[57] That is why only silence is the right attitude—not because the question has no answer, but because we realize the non-sense of the question itself, because there can be no questioning of the unquestionable (it would be a contradiction) and there can be no answer when there is no question.[58] Who can question the unquestionable? Certainly not the unquestionable itself; and from this questionable world there can be no question about what cannot be questioned. Anything that can be questioned is certainly not unquestionable. Thus the ontic silence of the Buddha.

In complete harmony with the central Christian doctrine of the *Incarnation*, the concept of *plērōma* (fullness, fulfillment) expresses the end of Man and of all creation.[59] Not only did the Redeemer come at the fullness of time,[60] but he let all those who believe in him be filled with his own fullness,[61] for of his fullness we have all received,[62] and in him the fullness of the deity dwells bodily.[63] It is then the fullness of God[64] that fills everything, though there is a distention, a period of expectation and hope until the restoration of all things.[65] Once the whole world is subjected unto him to whom all has been subjected, then he will subject himself fully to God so that God will be all in all.[66]

Apart from the possible hermetic, Gnostic and other uses of the word *plērōma*, Christian tradition has understood this message to mean being called to be as perfect as the heavenly Father;[67] being one with Christ[68] as he is one with his Father,[69] and thus becoming not like God, as the Tempter offered,[70] but God himself[71] through Man's union with the Son by the work and grace of the Spirit.[72]

Theiosis, divinization, was the technical word used during long centuries of Christian tradition, and the simplest formula was to say that God has become Man in order that Man might become God.[73]

The entire Christian economy is the transformation of the cosmos until the new heaven and the new earth,[74] which includes the resurrection of the flesh.[75] The destiny of Man is to become God, to reach the other shore where divinity dwells by means of the transformation that requires a new birth in order to enter the kingdom of heaven.[76] *Metanoia*, change of heart, of life and ultimately a passage from death to new life, was the central topic of Christ's proclamation,[77] for which John the Baptist, the forerunner, had already prepared the way.[78]

We should try now to understand what these words symbolize within their respective traditions.

Without *śūnyatā* thought is bound.[79] The fact is neither that the bound one is released nor the unbound one unreleased.[80] To realize the emptiness of all things is the culmination of all wisdom (*prajñā*), which leads to the discovery of the radical relativity of all things (*pratītyasamutpāda*), which begins the realization of *nirvāṇa*. In point of fact there is more a sense of equality than of hierarchy among these four notions.[81] We are not describing four steps, epistemological or ontological, but four ways of conveying one and the same realization: the realization that there is no-thing definitive in this world and that any other possibility, even the thought of it, is still linked with our 'this-worldly' experience and hence conditioned, dependent, not definitive—in a word, empty. Were it not for this emptiness things could not move; change would be impossible since material bodies could not move if there were no space between them. Emptiness is the very condition for the type of existence proper to things. And there is no-thing else, for any-thing else that could be would be affected by the same emptiness, by the very fact that we consider it possible and thus an object of our thought.

> There neither water nor earth,
> neither fire nor air can subsist,
> there the stars do not shine nor the sun illumine,
> there the moon does not brighten nor darkness exist.[82]

Without *plērōma* there would be no place for God, and human existence would make no sense. Man is more than Man; when he wants to be merely Man he degenerates into a beast.[83] He is destined for higher things.[84] Whenever he is disquiet,[85] whenever he searches for something, it is because God is already calling him.[86] Divine transcendence is safeguarded because Christian divinization is, properly speaking, more a 'filiation' than an undiscriminated fusion with the Father. The Christian Trinity is here the warranty for the appropriate distinction without separation. Man, and with him the entire universe, becomes one with the Son by the power and grace of the Spirit; as the Son he is one with the Father, but never becomes the Father. Even more, orthodox Christian thinking will stress in one way or another that while the Son *is* God of God, Light of Light, Man *becomes* one with the Son and so reaches the Godhead in and through the Son. Man's temporality ever remains a scar, as it were, in the very heart of his being. Divinization, Christian tradition will stress, does not mean human alienation precisely because Man is of divine nature.[87] Man is called upon to share God in a fuller way, to go home to his primordial nature and origin. Divinization reestablishes the image that had been distorted and makes Man what he is really called upon to become. Divine sonship is the truly human vocation. What Christ is by nature[88] is what Christ as Man's brother[89] has enabled Man to be and do by adoption (redemption): to share his sonship[90] in a new generation,[91] born again of water and the Spirit.[92]

3. RELIGIONS AND THE HUMANIZING OF MAN

It was a Greek who said Man is the measure of all things.[93] But it was another Greek who refuted him[94] and further affirmed it is God and not Man who is the measure of all things.[95] So that his disciple could say that Man, though mortal, should not satisfy himself with mortal things, but strive to become immortal.[96] They all might have remembered one of their ancestors saying: 'The idiosyncrasy of Man is his *daimōn*'.[97]

It was from Hebrew inspiration that it is written God created Man in his own image and likeness[98] and again from the same source that the sentence was often reversed and considered more a definition of God than a description of Man: God in the image of Man.[99]

It was a Jew influenced by Greek culture and by what his faith regarded as a unique event who wrote it was the divine Word dwelling with God that became flesh,[100] and a Roman who presented this same person as the Man.[101]

And it was a kṣatriya from the East who refused to speak about God and declined to indulge in merely theoretical speculations.[102] This same man was directly and exclusively concerned with giving concrete and effective advice about handling the human predicament.[103] Reacting against the religious inflation of his time and against the deleterious human condition of his neighbors, he centered all his life on showing how to be rid of the almost all-pervading human disquiet and anxiety, refusing even to undergird his teachings with any anthropology.[104] In this, he echoes the tradition of his own culture which had so strongly emphasized that:

The Man, indeed, is the All,
What has been and what is to be,[105]

because the primordial Man is the supreme reality.[106] No
wonder Buddhism was to flourish in the Humanistic soil par
excellence, the Confucian world, and in Chinese culture at
large.[107]

Following up the functional description of religion we
have already given, we may yet add that religion is the way in
which Man handles his human predicament in order to steer it
towards a somewhat better situation. Modern Man is acutely
aware of the urgency and difficulty of performing such a task.
Here the sketch of two great religious traditions could prove
of some value. With this we are saying that Comparative
Religion, far from being merely a comparison of religions or a
historical discipline, is in fact a study of ultimate human
problems—i.e., of religious situations—with the aid of more
than one religious tradition, so that by illuminating the concrete human predicament with the accumulated experience of
humankind we may be in a better position to understand it.

a. Buddhism, Christianity and Humanism

In this light we may now focus on the contemporary
Humanistic situation. For some decades Humanism has been a
powerful word.[108] It expresses a valuable myth that in the
traditionally Christian countries can be understood as a reaction against a certain devaluation of the human in favor of
something supernatural.[109] The 20th century has seen the
birth of all possible Humanisms: atheistic, scientific, new, classical, modern, mediaeval, social and even hyperbolical. Isolated voices have even been raised in favor of Hindu and
Buddhist Humanisms. It is difficult to decipher what is not a
Humanism, except some exaggerated and obviously inhuman
tendencies in several ideologies. Man is weary of certain dehumanizing trends in established religions. Humanism may be
a healthy reaction. Currently, modern ideologies and so-called
technocracies of every sort are also seen as dehumanizing

forces. Not only are a transcendental heaven and an eternal hell now viewed as dehumanizing, but society, techniques, modern cities, etc., are also seen as deleterious to Man. It is in this context that some would challenge traditional religions to really serve in this task of humanizing Man. And here we may add some reflections from the Buddhist and Christian viewpoint.

To begin with, religions are very sensitive about being dictated to from the outside or being told to serve anything, for they suppose themselves to be above any servitude. What matters is not 'saving' the human predicament according to Men's individual opinions, they will say, but seeing the situation as it really is in the light of the religious tradition. Perhaps what is called the 'Humanizing of Man' is nothing but his entanglement and damnation.

Avoiding these touchy attitudes, which come only from superficial approaches, we would like to approach the problem from the perspective of Comparative Religion or Philosophy of Religion as we defined it above.

The roughly seven thousand years of Man's historical memory show a common pattern present almost everywhere: the human desire for immortality. Overcoming death has always been a central religious and human concern. As to the means, religions differ. From the point of view of History of Religions one could be inclined to interpret the thrust toward divinization as a means for rescuing Man from the clutches of death as well as from the fear of nature or from the grip of the whole cosmos. In almost every religious tradition, the fundamental trait of divinization is immortality. Men are mortal and the Gods are immortal. The human predicament is that mortal Man must overcome his situation in the different ways offered by the most diverse religions. One way or another, traditional religions want to overcome the human condition by reaching the unconditioned. Divinization could appear phenomenologically as the unconditioning of the human condition. Man reaches the divine (which may be variously interpreted) once he has overcome his mortal condition. Christianity would be a peculiar instance of this attitude. Its doctrine of the Trinity lets it defend a total divinization (union with the Son) without destroying the God-Man difference.

Buddhism offers a different attitude. It does not want to uncondition but rather to decondition Man; it is not concerned with reaching transcendence but with overcoming immanence; it does not care as much about God as about deconditioning Man in a radical and ultimate way. Man has to cease being what he *is*, not in order to become another thing, not even God, but in order to totally negate the human and worldly situation. Buddhism shatters the human dream of any imaginable or thinkable survival.

Over against these two, present-day Secularism could represent a new attitude that considers time, i.e., the temporal universe, to be real and positive, and so not to be transcended.[110] Secularism does not mean unconditioning or deconditioning the human predicament, but soberly recognizing it as it appears. There is no escaping it or denying it. The driving force behind any Humanism is to make Man really Man and nothing but Man. And Man, Humanism would say, should banish any fear of worldly or superworldly powers. He has come of age, he need not fear being Man. But having overcome his fear of nature, of God and the Gods, Man now begins to fear himself and his societal reality. So the entire problem crops up all over again. We might ask, what is Man that he has to be made Man? Who is this being who needs to be made, to become what he is not—(yet ?).

b. Homo viator

An in-depth study of these three answers may perhaps furnish modern Man with a more elaborated model than any of the one-sided solutions so far proposed.[111] This would be a task of Comparative Religion.[112]

We may observe a double assumption: (1) Man is an unachieved being; (2) this achievement is the real Man.

The first part is almost a matter of course. The human status quo is never definitive. There is always room for change, repentance, hope, enlightenment, salvation, betterment and the like. The human predicament is infinite because it is not finite, not finished. Man is an open being: he 'ek-sists' by stretching out his being, along time and space at least.

The second assumption is less apparent and yet equally common to the three fundamental attitudes under analysis. No human tradition, religious or secular, endorses the alienation of Man. To radically convert Man into an altogether different being would not only be heterodox and foreign to any tradition, but nonsensical too. Any difference has meaning only within and over against an underlying identity. An absolute change is a contradiction in terms, for nothing would remain of what is supposed to have changed.

If Buddhism wants to annihilate Man, to decondition his human condition, to extinguish in him all *saṁsāric* existence, all remnants of creatureliness, it is because it presupposes that Man *is* not, that there is no *ātman*, so that the blowing out *(nirvāṇa)* of all spatio-temporal and experiential structures is then the 'true realization of Man's authentic "nature" '. The destruction of all our constructions is the real human liberation. And yet this does not conflict with the central orthodox Buddhist attitude of universal compassion *(karunā)*,[113] unlimited friendliness. You can embody a serene, joyful and even pragmatically effective loving attitude only if you have realized the *śūnyatā* of all things.

If Christianity wants to divinize Man, to let him share the divine nature and return through Christ to the Father, it is because it presupposes that the divine nature is the ultimate and most intimate constitution of Man.[114] Man is an offspring of God[115] and has to go back to the Father to fully realize what he is.[116] And yet this does not conflict with the distinction between God and Man, nor with the Christian emphasis on death and resurrection, new birth and total repentance. The risen Christ, like the risen Christian, is certainly a new creature,[117] but not another one *(aliud non alius)*. The person is the same.[118] In scholastic terms: *gratia non destruit, sed supponit et perfecit naturam.*[119] God does not become God, yet Man becomes what he is not yet.

Similarly, if Humanism wants to humanize Man by making

him recognize and accept his human condition, and to help
him resist the temptation of escaping into realms of unreality,
it is because it presupposes that the future of Man *is Man* and
that his authentic dignity consists in affirming his humanness
in spite of every allurement from above and below. Man has to
face his future with daring and dignity and, even when confronted with the absurd or the meaningless, he must accept
and affirm himself.[120] This attitude does not contravene the
Humanistic dogma that denies any substantial instance
superior to Man, for the secularized 'future' plays many of the
roles of the monotheistic God; but Humanism also requires a
proper belief in Man, which is a belief in the unseen.
Humanism demands of Man as heroic a posture as any traditional religion.

Nevertheless, despite all the structural similarities between these world views, we cannot overlook their differing
anthropologies, i.e., the different conceptions of Man and
ultimately of reality underlying them. Nothing is more barren
and dangerous than superficial agreements and merely tactical
compromises. The injunction to humanize Man, which practi-
cally everyone would admit, means various and opposite
things to different world views and religious traditions. The
real encounter comes when we cease to analyze structural
patterns and concentrate on the nature of the purpose itself.
What is humanizing? We can do no more here than ask the
question.

c. The Crossing of the Ways

If the study of religion means anything today, it has to
address itself to this problem. A whole new *methodic* is required because we can no longer pose the problem in the
limited and particularized way we have done until now, leaving
the world cut into cultural compartments. Even modern
Humanism is, by and large, as provincial and limited to its own
peculiar conception of Man and Reality as many of the more
traditional cultures it criticizes. Nobody can decide a priori
what it means to humanize Man, nor can this totally depend on

a single anthropology. It requires not a methodology but a
methodic of its own, which makes its way in and through the
mutual interaction and possible cross-fertilization of different
religions and cultures. A dialogical dialogue is necessary here.
This dialogical dialogue, which differs from a dialectical one,
stands on the assumption that nobody has access to the universal horizon of human experience, and that only by not postulating the rules of the encounter from a single side can Man
proceed towards a deeper and more universal understanding
of himself and thus come closer to his own realization. At this
point, to want to humanize Man according to some preconceived scheme, even if convincing for some, would amount to
repeating the same mistake so many religious traditions have
made in the conviction that they possessed the truth or had the
duty, and so the right, to proclaim their message of salvation.
No Man can be excluded from the task of humanizing Man; no
human tradition should be silent in this common task.

We may add a final thought, the distinction between
eclecticism and syncretism. The former is an uncritical mix-
ture of religious traditions and an agreement among them
obtained by chopping off all possible discrepancies in favor of
an amorphous common denominator. Syncretism is allowing
for a possible assimilation of elements by virtue of which these
elements cease to be foreign bodies, so that organic growth
within each tradition is possible, and the mutual fecundation
of religious traditions becomes a genuine option.[121]

Avoiding eclecticisms, but having in mind possible
interactions—although we should not minimize the existing
tensions, philosophical, theological or religious, between the
traditions under consideration—we may envision correc-
tions, warnings and complementarities that may not only allay
mutual suspicions and so often one-sided positions, but also
help cultivate a real human growth and thus contribute positively to a concrete humanization of human life on earth.

Let me indicate a few points for study. The central Buddhist concern is a timely reminder both to Christianity and to
every sort of Humanism that no amount of 'revelation' or

'reason' justifies manipulating Man under the guise of 'the will of God' or the 'demands of Reason' in order to steer him and the world to clearly defined goals. The ultimate goal is always so ineffable that it does not even exist. Buddhism is the thorough defense of the ultimate, absolutely ungraspable, mystery of existence. The mystery here is immanent.

The central Christian concern is a timely reminder to Buddhism and to all the Humanisms that no amount of self-effort and goodwill suffices to adequately handle the human predicament; we must remain constantly open to unexpected and unforeseeable eruptions of Reality itself, which Christians may want to call God or divine Providence. Christianity stands for the unselfish and authentic defense of the primordial rights of Reality, of which Man is not the master. The mystery here is transcendent.

Humanism, further, is a timely reminder to Buddhism and Christianity not only that traditional religions have often forgotten their own sayings—like the nonauthority of the Buddha,[122] who may even become the greatest obstacle to realizing one's own Buddha nature,[123] or like the Sabbath made for Man and not vice versa,[124] and the freedom of the children of God,[125] made free by truth itself[126]—but also that the humanizing of Man cannot lose sight of the concrete Man to be humanized. Pointing out the way or proclaiming the message will never suffice if the conditions are not given and worked for. Secularism is the awareness of Man's full responsibility upon coming of age. The mystery here is the intersection between immanence and transcendence.

Even at the risk of possible misunderstanding (should my words be interpreted only in one key), I would try to express what can be considered a true humanization of Man within the framework of these three major human traditions. Humanizing Man means to make him truly Man, but the expression is treacherous and ambivalent because this gerund is neither merely transitive nor merely intransitive. It is not as if someone else were humanizing Man or as if Man himself could achieve what he is not yet. Humanizing Man means rather this plunge into reality and participation in the overall destiny of all that is, which takes place inside and outside Man. It is a process by which Man becomes truly a person, sometimes abandoning the image he has of himself, dying, disappearing, transcending himself; other times affirming his being when it is threatened by alien forces, but in every case entering into a deeper *ontonomic* relationship with Reality—whatever this may be or not be. It is touching not only the shore of gentleness, power and wisdom but also the depths of despair, nothingness and death. It is to be all that Man is uniquely capable of; it cannot be compared to anything else. Each person is a unique knot in the universal net. It means to reach the heights of the Godhead if this is the model Man has of himself, provided such a vocation is not merely a wishful projection of lower unfulfilled desires. It means for Man to touch the shore of nothingness, provided he does not rest in that nonexisting place. It means to develop all the human potentialities, provided these are not artificially concocted dreams. It means finally to know and accept the human predicament and, at the same time, to recognize that this very human predicament carries with it the constant overcoming of all that Man is now.[127]

It is in this sense that today the sincere and totally (because disinterestedly) committed *studium* of religion, with all its attendant risks, uncertainties and joys, is perhaps one of the most authentic religious acts—at least for some of us.

NOTES

1. The nature of this chapter, I hope, justifies omitting so-called secondary literature—otherwise so helpful—and limiting quotations to just indicative samples. Most of the citations are taken from the author's books: *El Silencio del Dios* (Madrid: Guadiana, 1970) and *Humanismo y Cruz* (Madrid: Rialp, 1963).

2. Cf. R. Panikkar, 'Have "Religions" the Monopoly on *Religion?*', *Journal of Ecumenical Studies*, XI:3 (Summer, 1974), pp. 515-517.

3. I.e., the doctrine of the nonself or of the ultimate unsubstantiality of the being. Cf., for example, *Saṁyutta-nikāya* III, 66; *Dīgha-nikāya* II, 64 sq.; *Milindapanha* II, 1, 1 (or 251); II, 2, 1; III 5, 6; *et al.*

4. The four noble truths or *aryasaccāni* (in Sanskrit, *āryasatyāni*), namely: the universal fact of sorrow, the different cravings as the cause of sorrow, the stopping of all cravings as the stopping of sorrow and the eightfold path leading out of sorrow: right vision, right intention, right discourse, right behavior, right livelihood, right effort, right memory and right concentration. Cf. *Saṁyutta-nikāya* V, 420 sq.

5. I.e., all is sorrow. Cf. *Dhammapada* XX, 6 (Nr. 278). Suffering, un-easiness, turmoil, etc., are other versions of *duḥkham* (from the root *duṣ*, deteriorate).

6. Cf. *Mahāparinibbāna-sutta* VI, 10; III, 66; *et al.* Cf., incidentally, Phil. 2:12: 'You must work out your own salvation in fear and trembling.'

7. Gen. 1:1 sq.; 1:31; *et al.*

8. Cf. Lk. 2:11; Acts 13:23; *et al.*

9. Cf. Jn. 1:14; *et al.*

10. Cf. Deut. 6:5.

11. Cf. Mt. 22:37-40.

12. The Pāli *taṇhā* corresponds to the Sanskrit *tṛṣṇa*, meaning thirst. Besides the text already quoted, cf. *Aṅguttara-nikāya* III, 416; IV, 400; *Saṁyutta-nikāya* I, 1; I, 8; *Majjhima-nikāya* I, 6; II, 256; *Itivuttaka* 30; 50; 58; 105; *et al.*

13. The New Testament term is *epithymia*, which Latin theology translated by *concupiscentia*. Cf. 1 Jn. 2:16-17; 2 Pet. 2:18; Gal. 5:16; Rom. 6:12; 2 Tim. 3:6; *et al.*

14. Cf. *Majjhima-nikāya* III, 6: 'The Tathāgata limits himself to show the path'; *et al.* (cf. also *Majjhima-nikāya* I, 83).

15. Cf. Jn. 10:9; 14:6; *et al.*

16. Cf. *Milindapanha* 326; *et al.*

17. Cf. Jn. 16:8 sq.; 17:9 sq.; *et al.*

18. Cf. *Udāna* V, 5: 'As, O bhikkhus, the great ocean has but one single taste, the salty taste, even so, O bhikkhus, the discipline of the teaching has but one single taste, the taste of liberation. That the discipline of the teaching, O bhikkhus, has a single taste, the taste of liberation, this is, O bhikkhus, the sixth marvelous and extraordinary thing of the discipline of the teaching.' Cf. the same metaphor in CU VI, 13 for a different, but related, teaching. Cf. also Jn. 8:36; 1 Pet. 2:16; Rom. 8:21; *et al.*, for the Christian side.

19. The word is not exclusively Buddhist, as is proved by the BG II, 72; VI, 15; the MB XIV, 543; *et al.*; and confirmed by the discussions on the non-Buddhist meanings of the term in *Digha-nikāya* I, 3; 19; etc.

20. The word is on the one hand the Greek rendering of the hebrew *yeshuah*, *yesha* and *teshuah*, and on the other the Christian rendering of the

same word of classical antiquity; often ambivalent, i.e., applied to Gods and Men alike.

21. Cf. *Saṁyutta-nikāya* II, 68.

22. I.e., 'of all this-worldly elements', 'of all creatureliness' one could venture to translate. Cf. *ibid.* I, 136.

23. Cf. *ibid.* I, 210.

24. Cf. *ibid.* I, 39.

25. Cf. the etymology of *nirvāṇa*: from the intransitive verb *nirvā*, be extinct, consumed. The root *vā* means blow, *vāta* means wind (cf. *spiritus, pneuma*). *Nirvāṇa* is the extinction of all combustible (mortal, contingent, temporal) material.

26. Cf. *Kathavatthu* XIX, 6.

27. Cf. *Itivuttaka* II, 6 (or 43); *Udāna* VIII, 3.

28. Cf. *Udāna* VIII, 1.

29. Cf. Nāgārjuna, *Mūlamādhyamikakārikā* XXV, 1 sq.

30. Cf. Candrakīrti, *Prasannapadā* XXIV, *passim*.

31. Cf. the entire chapter III or *suññatavagga* of *Majjhima-nikāya*.

32. Cf. the famous parable of the man wounded by the arrow who dies, having wasted his time inquiring after such unnecessary details as who shot it and why, in *Majjhima-nikāya* I, 426 sq.; *Aṅguttara-nikāya* IV, 67 sq.

33. Cf. *Majjhima-nikāya* III, 254, where concentration is called void, signless and aimless.

34. *Udāna* VIII, 3. Cf. also Candrakīrti, *Prasannapadā* XXV, 3 (ed. La Vallée Poussin; tr. R.H. Robinson, p. 521): 'Nirvāṇa is defined as un-abandoned, unattained, unannihilated, non-eternal, unextinguished, una-risen.'

35. This could be considered the quintessence of Nāgārjuna's insight.

36. Cf. the important concept of *asaṁskṛta*, the nonconstructed. The notion of *akata (akṛta)*, the not-done, -made, -created, stands in contraposition to the *saṁskṛta*, the constructed, of the Indian tradition. Cf. *Dhammapada* VII, 8 (97).

37. Cf. Phil. 1:28.

38. Cf. 2 Cor. 7:10.

39. Cf. 1 Th. 5:9; *et al.*

40. Cf. Heb. 2:10.

41. Cf. Heb. 5:9.

42. Cf. 1 Pet. 1:9-10.

43. Cf. Jn. 4:22.

44. Cf. Acts 16:17.

45. Cf. Acts 13:26; *et al.*

46. Cf. Lk. 1:77.

47. Cf. Lk. 2:11 and the very name Jesus *(Yoshua)* which means salvation.

48. Cf. Mt. 1:21; Acts 5:31.

49. Cf. Acts 4:12.

50. The root *śū* (*śvid*) means 'swell', and the term *śūnya* (empty or void) exists already in ancient pre-Buddhist and non-Buddhist literature. Cf. AV XIV, 2, 19; SB II, 3, 1, 9; TB II, 1, 2, 12; and many Upaniṣads. An interesting compound is *śūnyāgāra*, the deserted, empty house (JabU VI), signifying the house where the *samnyasis* or Hindu monks were supposed to live (or also in a dwelling-place of the God, a temple: *devagṛha*). Cf. also MaitU VI, 10.

51. There is no need to stress that *plērōma*—i.e., that which fills (up)—is of pre-Christian origin and has its full meaning in Greek literature.

52. Cf. the beginning of Nāgārjuna's *Mūlamadhyamikakārikā* I, 1: 'Neither out of themselves, nor out of something else, nor out of any cause, do existing things arise.'

53. Cf. the expression *svabhāvaśūnyatā* (emptiness of [in] its own being) as one mode of emptiness described in the *Pañcaviṁsarisāhasrikā* (one of the later Prajñapāramitā-sūtras), or the expression *svabhāvaśūnya* as the quintessence of the *Prajñāpāramitā*, 1 (the so-called *Heart-sūtra*). Cf. also the *dharmaśūnyatā* of Śāntideva's *Sikṣāsamuccaya* XIV, 242 and the *śūnyabhutaḥ* (void of being) of the MaitU VI, 23.

54. The simile of the other shore is recurrent in Buddhist literature. Cf. *Aṅguttara-nikāya* II, 24; IV, 13; IV, 160; *Itivuttaka* 69; *Saṁyutta-nikāya* IV, 175; *Prajñāpāramitā-sūtra* IX; *et al.*

55. Cf. Nāgārjuna, *Mūlamādhyamikakārikā* XXV, 19.

56. Were there any difference between the two, this would be *saṁsāra* or *nirvāṇa* of some third thing, each of which is contradictory.

57. Cf. *Lalitavistara* XIII, 175 sq. *Majjhima-nikāya* I, 297, stresses that the world is empty (in pāli, *suñña*) of self and of what pertains to the self (*attā* and *attaniya*). Cf. also *Saṁyutta-nikāya* IV, 54 and 296; *et al.*

58. Cf. *Saṁyutta-nikāya* III, 189.

59. Cf. Eph. 4:13; *et al.*

60. God sent his Son at the fullness of time *(chronos)* (Gal. 4:4), but in the fullness of times *(kairos)* he will gather all things in Christ (Eph. 1:10).

61. Cf. Eph. 1:23.

62. Cf. Jn. 1:16.

63. Col. 2:9.

64. Cf. Eph. 3:19.

65. Cf. Acts 3:21.

66. Cf. 1 Cor. 15:28.

67. Cf. Mt. 5:48.

68. Cf. Jn. 15:1 sq.

69. Cf. Jn. 6:56-57; 17:23; *et al.*

70. Cf. Gen. 3:5.

71. Cf. Jn. 1:12 (and, with qualifications, 10:34-35); *et al.*

72. Cf. Jn. 14:17; 15:26; *et al.*

73. Cf. Clement of Alexandria, *Proptrepticus* I, 9 (here using *theopoiein* which generally referred to the making of idols); Gregory of Nazianzus, *Oratio theologica* III, 19 (P. G., 36, 100); Athanasius: αὐτὸς γὰρ φνηνθρώπησεν ἵνα ἥμεις θεοποιη θῶμεν; 'Ipse siquidem homo factus est, ut nos dii efficeremur', (For he was made Man that we might be made God) *De Incarnatione Verbi* 54 (P. G., 25, 192); *Oratio 4 contra arrianos* VI (P. G., 26, 476); Augustine, *Sermo* 128 (P. L., 39, 1997); *Sermo de Nativitate* 3 and 11 (P. L., 38, 99 and 1016); 'Propter te factus est temporalis, ut tu fias aeternus', says Augustine in his lapidary style, *Epist. Io.* II, 10 (P. L., 35, 1994); 'Quod est Christus, erimus Christiani', repeats Cyprian, *De idolorum vanitate* XV (P. L., 4, 582); *et al.*

74. Cf. Rev. 21:1.

75. Cf. 1 Cor. 15:12 sq.

76. Cf. Jn. 3:3 sq.

77. Cf. Mt. 4:17; *et al.*

78. Cf. Mt. 3:2; *et al.*

79. Cf. Śāntideva, *Bodhicaryāvatāra* IX, 49.

80. Cf. Candrakīrti, *Prasannapadā* XVI, 8 (ed. La Vallée Poussin, p. 293).

81. *Prajñā, śūnyatā, pratītyasamutpāda, nirvāṇa.*

82. *Udāna* I, 10.

83. Cf. the famous saying of Pascal, *Pensées*, 358: 'L'homme n'est ni ange ni bête, et le malheur veut que qui veut faire l'ange fait la bête.'

84. Cf. the oft-quoted passage, 'Agnosce, O Christiane, dignitatem tuam, et divinae consors factus naturae, noli in veterem vilitatem degeneri conversatione redire. Memento cuius capitis et cuius corpis sis membrum', Leo I, *Sermo* 21, 3 (P. L., 54, 192-193).

85. Cf. the famous Augustinian 'irrequietum est cor nostrum donec requiescat in te'. *Confess.* I, 1, 1.

86. Cf. Maximus Confessor, *Ambigua*, 'God has inserted in the human heart the desire of him' (P. G., 91, 1312); or, accepting the idea that a purified *epithymia* (consupiscence) can become the burning desire of him, *Quaest. ad Thal.* (P. G., 90, 269). Cf. the Christian commentary on Jn. 6:44: 'Nemo te quaerere valet nisi qui prius invenerit', Bernard of Clairvaux, *De diligendo Deo* VII, 22 (P. L., 182, 987); also, 'Console toi, tu ne me chercherais pas, si tu ne m'avais pas trouvé.' Pascal, *Pensées*, 553.

87. Cf. 2 Pet. 1:4; *et al.*

88. Cf. Rom. 8:29; *et al.*

89. Cf. Heb. 2:11; *et al.*

90. Cf. Gal. 4:5; *et al.*

91. Cf. 1 Jn. 2:29; *et al.*

92. Cf. Jn. 3:5; *et al.*

93. Πάντων Χεημάτων μέτρον ἄνθρωπος, Protagoras, *Frag. 1.*

94. Cf. Plato, *Cratylus*, 386a; *Theatetus*, 152a.

95. Cf. Plato, *Laws* IV (716 c).

96. Cf. Aristotle, *Nicomachean Ethics* X, 7 (1177 b 31).

97. Literally: 'ηθος ἀνθρώπῳ δαίμων—'The ethos to Man (is his) *daimōn.*' Heraclitus, *Frag.* 119.

98. Cf. Gen. 1:26-27.

99. This could be said to be the theological justification of all Humanisms of a biblical origin.

100. Cf. Jn. 1:14.

101. Cf. Jn. 19:5.

102. Cf. the famous *avyakṛtavastuni*, or unutterable things, which the Buddha refused to answer. Cf. the *vacchagotta saṁyuttam* (*Saṁyutta-nikāya* III, 33), *avyakata saṁyuttam* (*Saṁyutta-nikāya* IV, 44), *cūlamāluṅkya sutta* (*Majjhima-nikāya* 63), the *aggivacchagotta sutta* (*Majjhima-nikāya* 72), etc.

103. Cf., for instance, Buddha's refusal to elaborate on the nature of karma because the only thing that matters is getting rid of it. Cf. *Aṅguttara-nikāya* II, 80; *Digha-nikāya* III, 138; *Saṁyutta-nikāya* III, 103.

104. That the Buddha 'has no theories' (*Majjhima-nikāya* I, 486) is a constant idea in the Buddhist canon, later converted in the Madhyāmika into the central message of Buddhism.

105. RV X, 90, 2.

106. Cf. SU III, 8 sq.; *et al.*

107. This reference to the Chinese world is meant to signify that no complete and valid discourse on humanization can take place today without including what is perhaps the most humane of all cultures, whose ideal has always been the perfect Man. Cf. a single example, which may well be considered representative of more than one tradition: 'Therefore the Perfect Man makes his spirit and mind penetrate the limitless and cannot be impeded by limits, pushes to the utmost the sight and hearing of eye and ear and cannot be contrained by sound and forms—because he identifies with the self voidness of the myriad things. Thus, things cannot hinder his spirit-intelligence.' Seng-Chao, *Emptiness of the Non-Absolute* (Chao-lun III; tr. R.H. Robinson).

108. No point in giving here a bibliography that would cover more pages than our entire chapter.

109. Cf. the well-known *splendida vitia* of Augustine for the 'virtues' of those not reborn in baptism. And again, 'Bene currunt; sed in via non currunt. Quanto plus currunt, plus errant; quia a via recedunt', *Sermo* 141, c. 4, nr. 4 (P. L., 38, 777). Or again, 'maius opus est ut ex impio iustus fiat, quam creare caelum et terram', *In Ioh.* tr. 72, nr. 3 (P. L., 35, 1823), commented upon by Thomas, 'Bonum gratiae unius maius est quam bonum naturae totius universi' (*Sum. theol.* I-II, q. 113, a. 9, c. et ad 2), and again, developed

in his own way by Meister Eckhart in his *Serm. lat.* II, 2 (*Lateinische Werke* IV, 16, n. 10); *et al.*

110. Cf. the etymological hint: *Saeculum* is certainly not the *kosmos*, but rather the *aeōn*, the life span (cf. the Sanskrit *āyus*), i.e., the temporal aspect of the world.

111. We say one-sided because it cannot be denied that the traditional answers have not taken into account the whole of the human horizon; in our kairological moment, this is imperative.

112. Needless to say, we can only indicate in a general way how fundamental research on this problem could be started.

113. In point of fact, *karuṇā* and *śūnyatā* are the two pillars of Mahāyāna Buddhism, and many texts link them.

114. Cf. the well-known 'tu autem eras interior intimo meo et superior summo meo' of Augustine (*Confessions* III, 6, 11). Cf. also Thomas, *Sum. theol.*, I, q. 8, a. 1; I, q. 105, a. 5; Calvin, *Institutiones christianae religionis* III, 7: 'Quod si nostri non sumus, sed Domini . . . ergo ne vel ratio nostra, vel voluntas in consiliis nostris factisque dominetur (. . .) Nostri non sumus: ergo quoad licet obliviscamur nosmetipsos ac nostra omnia. Rursum, Dei sumus: illi ergo vivamus et moriamur,' (*Opera Calvini*, ed. Brunsvigae, 1864, vol. 2, col. 505-506); not to mention the mystics.

115. Cf. Acts 17:28.

116. Cf. Jn. 17:22-26; *et al.*

117. Cf. 2 Cor. 5:17; Gal. 6:15; Eph. 4:24; Col. 3:10; *et al.*

118. Interestingly enough, the Buddhist intuition of *nairātmyavāda* tallies in an astounding way with the Christian doctrine of the *perichōrēsis* (*circumincessio*).

119. Cf. Thomas, *Sum. theol.*, I, q. 1, a. 8 ad 2; I, q. 2, a. 2 ad 1; although Aquinas does not use the literal words of this later famous principle.

120. Any Humanism entails an affirmation of Man that transcends the 'Man' who affirms it.

121. Cf. R. Panikkar, "Some Notes on Syncretism and Eclecticism related to the Growth of Human Consciousness" in *Religious Syncretism in Antiquity. Essays in Conversation with Geo Widengren* edited by Birger A. Pearson, Missoula, Montana (Scholars Press), 1975, pp. 47-60.

122. A recurrent theme of the Buddha's teachings is that they do not have authority of their own, but only inasmuch as the hearer experiences them as conveying a real message of liberation. Cf. the Buddhist tradition: 'Those who fantasize about the Buddha, who is beyond fancies and imperishable, are all slain by fancy and do not see the *Tathāgata*' (Candrakīrti, *Prasannapadā* XXII, 15 [ed. La Vallée Poussin, tr. R.H. Robinson, p. 448]).

123. This goes to the extreme of: 'Kill the Buddha if you happen to meet him!' *Taishō Tripitaka* 47,500b (apud K. Ch'en, *Buddhism in China*. Princeton: Princeton University Press, 1964, p. 358).

124. Cf. Mk. 2:27.
125. Cf. Rom. 8:21; *et al.*
126. Cf. Jn. 8:32.
127. Cf. the *Sermo I* of C.G. Jung's *VII Sermones ad mortuos* printed privately in 1916 and published as Appendix to his Autobiography: *Erinnerungen, Träume, Gedanken* edited by A. Jaffe, (Olten-Freiburg: Walter) 1972, pp. 389 sq. Some excerpts: "Das Nichts oder die Fülle nennen wir das *Pleroma* [where the Greek-Christian terminological bias is apparent]. Dort drin hört denken und sein auf, denn das ewige und unendliche hat keine eigenschaften." [*sic* with the capitals]

LAUS DEO VIRGINEQUE MATRI

INDEX

102

understanding, 8, 9, 10, 16.
Divinity, as act, 70; in Man, 81, 87;
nature of, 87.
Dogma, 60; cf. Belief; and belief, 7,
19, 21, 35; development of, 70,
71; and other traditions, 17; and
truth, 7.

Eckart, Meister, 97.
Eclecticism, 89.
Ecumenism, 2; cf. Dialogue,
Encounter; ecumenical, 3, 4;
spirit of, 3.
Emptiness, cf. *Śūnyatā*.
Encounter, religious, cf. Dialogue
Tradition; and epoché, 13, 42, 43,
44, 46, 47; and history, 28;
necessity of, 61, 69; and
philosophy, 51; as religious, 26,
27, 30, 34, 37, 54; and theology,
31, 33; and truth, 37.
Epiphany, Christ as, 16; of God, 14,
16; Kṛṣṇa as, 9, 14, 16;
multiplicity of, 15.
Eopché, and belief, 42, 43, 45, 46,
47; and encounter, 13, 42, 43,
44, 46; and faith, 41, 42, 43, 45.
Eschatology, 16, 56, 70.
Eucharist, 71.
Experience, Christian, 59; and
convictions, 47; as
cosmotheandric, 4; of dialogue,
17, 20; of faith, 21; human, 77,
79, 84, 89; of life, 7; religious,
16, 20, 66, 67, 68, 69.

Faith, cf. Belief; as act, 7, 21, 68;
and belief, 2, 7, 9, 12, 17, 18, 19,
20, 21, 22, 35, 42, 43; as
constitutive, 2, 21; and epoché,
41, 42, 43, 45, 48, 49; function
of, 18, 22; living of, 6, 13, 30;
one's own, 12, 13; of others, 12,
16, 20; as personal, 13, 14;
risking of, 13, 50; and truth, 8-9,
12; and universality, 6, 13, 18,
21.
Fall, 77.
Father, 19, 81, 82, 87.
Fathers of Church, 58, 62, 70.

Gadamer, H.G., 23.
Gentiles, 59, 68.
Gītā, 54.
Gnostics, 63, 81.
God, belief in, 7, 8, 9, 19, 42, 48;
concepts of, 6, 63; as creator, 45,
77, 83; epiphanies of, 14, 16;
existence of, 8; fullness of, 80;
and growth, 70; kingdom of, 63,
81; love for, 10, 11, 77; love of,
14; and man, 14, 15, 36, 63;
names of, 14; non-belief in, 7;
non-existence of, 8; Spirit of, 63;
transcendence of, 15, 30.
Gospel, and dialogue, 11.
Grace, 21, 47, 81, 87.
Greeks, 17, 59, 62.
Gregory of Nazianzus, 95.

Hacker, P., 74.
Hebrews, cf. Jews.
Heraclitus, 96.
Heresy, 14, 30, 64.
Hermeneutic(s), 4, 30, 57; and
dialogue, 33; principles of, 31,
32, 62.
Hinduism, 28, 29, 47, 55, 56, 57,
64, 68, 72, 73, 84.
Hippolytus, 59.
History, and Christ, 17; dynamism
of, 5, 15; and eschatology, 16, 56;
of religions, 18, 22, 30, 85; and
traditions, 27, 28, 29, 56, 63.
Holy Spirit, belief in, 7, 19; grace
of, 81, 82, 83.
Homology, 33, 34.
Humanity, predicament of, 76-91.
Humanism, 72, 84, 86, 87, 88, 89,
90.
Husserl, 46, 51.

Idols, 30, 44.
Ignorance, 77.
Incarnation, 77, 80.
Islam, cf. Muslims.

Jaffe, A., 98.
Jerome, 28.
Jews, 17, 59, 68, 71, 83.
John, 59, 60.